MW00784384

# Quiet Works

**Also by Joseph McCormack**

*BRIEF: Make a Bigger Impact by Saying Less*
*NOISE: Living and Leading When Nobody Can Focus*

# Quiet Works

making **silence** the
secret ingredient
of the workday

## Joseph McCormack

Matt Holt Books
An Imprint of BenBella Books, Inc.
Dallas, TX

Matt Holt is an imprint of BenBella Books, Inc.
10440 N. Central Expressway
Suite 800
Dallas, TX 75231
benbellabooks.com
Send feedback to feedback@benbellabooks.com

*BenBella* and *Matt Holt* are federally registered trademarks.

Printed in the United States of America
10 9 8 7 6 5 4 3 2 1

Library of Congress Control Number: 2024009437
ISBN 9781637745694 (hardcover)
ISBN 9781637745700 (electronic)

Editing and copyediting by Lydia Choi
Proofreading by Becky Maines and Lisa Story
Text design and composition by Jordan Koluch
Cover design by Alison Hall / TheBarnCompany.com
Cover image © Shutterstock / sanua9
Printed by Lake Book Manufacturing

---

**Special discounts for bulk sales are available.**
**Please contact bulkorders@benbellabooks.com.**

*To Julie, my wife, who always loves me and cares for me. From the very beginning, you have believed in me and inspired me with your kindness, intelligence, and positivity. I'm so honored to be on this mission together.*

*To the quiet professionals that I serve. Thanks for your relentless pursuit of excellence and constant concern for character, discipline, and discretion. What problems can't you solve by spending some time in silence?*

# Contents

*Foreword by Joseph L. Votel*                                                        ix

*Preface*                                                                            xi


**Part One: Our Noisy World Just Gets Noisier**

1. The Lay of the (Loud) Land                                                         5
2. The Workplace Is Sick (and We Are, Too)                                           13
3. TMI, TMC (Too Much Information,
   Too Much Collaboration)                                                           23
4. Thoughtless, Scattered Leaders Scare Us                                           33
5. AI Is Making Things a Lot Worse                                                   43


**Part Two: Quiet Isn't What You Think**

6. My Turning Point: How I Realized
   Quiet Was the Missing Piece                                                       63
7. Words of Wisdom and Why We Run from Quiet                                         69
8. Knowing What Quiet Is and Isn't
   (It's *Not* a Technique; It's an Appointment)                                     81

## Part Three: Quiet Practices at Work

9. Principles and Practices: Defining What You Believe
   Will Shape How You Behave ............................................. 91
10. Permission to Pause: The Discipline to Do Nothing ........ 97
11. Leave Me Alone—It Can Wait!
    (Not Everything Is an Emergency) ................................... 109
12. The Quiet Works Toolkit:
    Six Ways to Make Quiet Time Stick ................................ 119
13. Tech Time-Outs to Reclaim Your Day ........................... 141

## Part Four: Quiet Places and Programs

14. Creating a Culture of Quiet ........................................... 151
15. Quiet Works for Leaders—Going It Alone .................... 163
16. Quiet Works for Teams—A Bottom-Up Approach .......... 179
17. Quiet Works for Coaching—
    The Missing Puzzle Piece for Breakthroughs ................ 187
18. Semi-Silent Summits: Why Quiet Works for Off-Sites .... 197
19. Quiet Works for BRIEF Communicators ....................... 205
20. An Essay: Imagining the Quiet Workplace ................... 219

## Part Five: Quiet Challenges

21. Professional Leaders Predict a Payoff—QCO:
    Questions, Challenges, and Observations ...................... 233
22. Challenges to Get You Started ..................................... 239

Acknowledgments .............................................................. 245
Notes .................................................................................. 247

# *Foreword*

As the commander of the US Special Operations Command and the US Central Command from 2014 to 2019, I found myself in consecutive leadership positions that were highly demanding on my time and cognitive capabilities. The pace of our operations was fierce. The day-to-day problems had layers of complexity and nuance. The impact of decision-making was extraordinary. The consequences came swiftly and, in some cases, with deadly effects. Keeping everyone informed, up and down the chain of command, was a constant requirement. The pace of change and uncertainty injecting themselves into the environment was unrelenting.

I had to find a way to exert control over my schedule, my staff, and our operating method to preserve my energy and ensure that tasks that only I could do were done well and the organization could stay focused on its mission. The military is excellent at developing leaders who can make good decisions. Still, we pay little attention to how we train them to manage crushing calendars, a constant deluge of information, and the need to reduce the external distractions that get us off track.

This extraordinary book by my friend Joe McCormack is an excellent tool for leaders and workers in the public and private sectors dealing with situations similar to where I served as a senior military officer. More importantly, these are tools that anyone can apply to stay focused and get a job done.

I met Joe several years ago as the Joint Special Operations Command commander. At the time, Joe came to talk with us about strategic messaging and narratives. I learned in our first engagement about his book *BRIEF: Make a Bigger Impact by Saying Less*. Together with The BRIEF Lab, he helped generations of military leaders master the skills needed for concise and practical strategic communications. I was a beneficiary through improving my skills but also, more importantly, through the officers and noncommissioned officers who served alongside me. He doubled down on his success with *NOISE: Living and Leading When Nobody Can Focus*, a guide with practical tips on managing distraction-filled environments.

This latest work, *Quiet Works: Making Silence the Secret Ingredient of the Workday*, completes the circle. It does so by offering valuable and easily applied skills to set conditions in our work lives to be more strategic, more intentional, and better enabled to reduce the cacophony of distractions that disrupt our efforts to get work done. A recent study published by the University of California suggested that we spend only twelve minutes on a task before we are interrupted by an email, a colleague, or some other external distraction. The time to get back on task is nearly double that: twenty-five minutes. Significantly, distractions increase stress, frustration, and time pressure, and they reduce effort. The need for an individualized approach to managing distractions at work is readily evident, making this book timely and necessary. I cannot think of anyone who would not benefit from a better approach to reducing the daily distractions in our working lives.

I hope you enjoy reading this book and applying the tools.

Joseph L. Votel
General, US Army (Retired)

# *Preface*

've spent the past decade on a journey toward "quiet." It started with my first book, *BRIEF: Make a Bigger Impact by Saying Less.* For a long time, I had been thinking about the necessity of being clear and concise in a world flooded with information. If we don't get to the point, we get dismissed. So, in 2013, I wrote a step-by-step guide on how to say what we need to say quickly. (And yes, I kept it brief.)

I never really thought there would be a second book. But five years later, I was moved to write again. I couldn't stop thinking about the abundant information bombarding us every day. As we navigate through bustling corridors of our professional lives, we find ourselves drowning in a sea of noise, distractions, and constant demands for our attention.

The modern work environment, once hailed as a hub of productivity and innovation, has transformed into a cacophony of chatter, ringing phones, pinging emails, and relentless interruptions. For a while now, it's affected our ability to work and live in a healthy way. And so, in 2019, I wrote *NOISE: Living and Leading When Nobody Can Focus* to help people push back against the rising tide of useless information and distraction.

Then, as I prepared to launch *NOISE*, COVID-19 hit. Irony of ironies! As huge numbers of people were forced to stay home, a hush fell over the world. (Google "lockdown" and "quiet," and a spate of 2020 articles marveling at the new silence pops up.) And as people began working remotely, they discovered silence and solitude were the secret ingredients that had been missing all along. With our newfound quiet, we became more productive than ever . . .

. . . and happier . . .

. . . and healthier.

Yet nothing lasts forever. Today, while many of us still work from home, there's a big push to bring people back to the office—at least part of the time. Many employees commute to their workplaces one or more days a week, and this trend is likely to continue. We now have a unique opportunity. A once-every-hundred-years pandemic that changed our way of life is (barely) in our rearview mirror, and we are finding a new normal as professionals and as people.

As more businesses continue moving to a hybrid work model, it's essential that we understand the real cost of allowing too much noise to disrupt our organizations. We cannot—must not—underestimate the benefits of building work sanctuaries where focusing, thinking, deep work, and genuine collaboration can thrive.

All of which brings me to *this* book. It is my hope that *Quiet Works: Making Silence the Secret Ingredient of the Workday* will help professionals realize we can hold on to the lessons we learned during the past few years and keep pushing to evolve and reimagine the workplace, eradicating wasted time, careless collaboration, and thoughtless work that's still rampant there and inserting pockets of quiet time to work alone.

In *Quiet Works*, I'll talk about why we struggle with noise in today's workplace. From open office layouts to the constant barrage of digital distractions, we will uncover the hidden costs of our noisy work environments and the toll they take on our ability to think, communicate, and innovate effectively.

This book is an encouraging call to action, not just an admiration of the problem. We'll explore all the simple, practical ways that a culture of quiet can renew, refresh, and refocus us to be empowered to do our best work. We'll delve into proven strategies, tools, and techniques that leaders and teams can leverage to create that culture. We'll look at real-life examples and compelling research that shows how quiet workplaces can revolutionize our professional lives and transform our organizations.

Looking back, all the dots connect: *BRIEF* is about clear communication, *NOISE* is about the peril of overcommunication, and *Quiet Works* is about the periodic need to stop talking altogether. Thoughtful communication requires quiet time to prepare; thoughtless communication creates noise.

All my books to date are about overcoming serious challenges and enjoying tangible rewards:

- It's hard to get to the point, but it is so relieving to others when you do.
- It's tough managing the nonstop noise, but so fulfilling to regain focus.
- And it's difficult to stop the 24/7 urge to digest and disseminate information, yet so clarifying, restful, and restorative when you can find a time and place for silence.

Whether you are a CEO seeking to improve your team's focus, culture, and productivity, an individual contributor striving to find your creative flow, or a manager looking to create a more conducive work environment, *Quiet Works* is for you. It is a clear call for change, an invitation to embrace silence as a catalyst for success in the modern workplace.

Join me on this journey—one that will change the face of the modern work environment forever. Together we can reclaim our ability to think deeply, communicate effectively, and create remarkable work in a world that is increasingly drowning in noise. It's time to silence the distractions,

## Preface

elevate our work, and forge a new path toward a more focused, meaning-ful, and productive future.

Now I'll hush, so you can get to reading!

> All of humanity's problems stem from man's inability to sit qui-etly in a room alone.
>
> —Blaise Pascal

# Quiet Works

# PART ONE

# OUR NOISY WORLD JUST GETS NOISIER

Once you get used to the constant bombardment of noise, it just looks and feels like normal life. Our brains are locked (tricked or hacked, really) into a mode of insatiable information consumption that becomes a hard habit to break. We subconsciously redefine working as being always on and won't permit ourselves or anyone to turn it off for fear we might miss something critical. With endless sources of information and constant connectivity, the reach of noise is seemingly endless morning to night, wherever we go. Good luck getting off the hamster wheel.

## Chapter 1

# The Lay of the (Loud) Land

W e live in a world of relentless noise. No matter where we are or what we're doing, information comes at us from all directions. It never stops. And it's not just annoying; it's deeply harmful.

Think about the many ways noise infiltrates our days. We're held captive by screens morning to night, from computers and smartphones to televisions and tablets. (Heck, even our watches are screens!) We spend hours on social media. We're in and out of meetings and conference calls all day. Emails overload our inboxes. We constantly chat, text, and message.

Somehow, when we weren't paying attention, noise took over our life.

It hasn't always been this way. (Remember?) But as technology has evolved over the past few decades, constant connectivity has become the norm. In fact, if you're from a younger generation you've never experienced a non-digital life.

You may not have considered the very real cost of noise and the toll it takes on not only your well-being but also your effectiveness, productivity, and agency. I'm very sorry to break it to you, but you are almost certainly being hampered by noise in big and small ways.

*Nowhere is this more evident than in the American workplace.*

The modern workplace reminds me of a hive of bees. There's constant activity, the constant presence of coworkers, and, of course, a constant audible buzz.

Perhaps this seems like a good thing, or at least a neutral thing. But it's not. Humans are not bees, and the work we do is very different. While we *do* need connection and collaboration from time to time, some of us need it less than others. (Introverts, I'm looking at you.)

Virtually everyone needs periods of quiet to organize their thoughts, challenge themselves, and do meaningful work. Yet the noise bombarding us keeps us in a state of inner chaos. The unending distraction makes it nearly impossible to focus, complete tasks, and move forward.

## The (Life-Ruining) Risks of Noise

There's no doubt living with too much noise decreases our quality of life. It ruins our attention spans, curbs efficiency, disrupts our work–life balance, diminishes our mental health and general well-being, and prevents us from thriving. This is bad news for individuals, but it spells disaster for organizations. A company where no one can focus, innovate, and execute is a company that's doomed to die a slow and painful death—or perhaps a sudden one.

It sounds depressing and dire because it is. Here are some examples of the consequences of working while engulfed in a tsunami of noise:

- **You lose the ability to concentrate and do deep work.** No one can dig deep and focus when they're interrupted by emails, phones ringing, too many meetings, conversations from the next cubicle over, and any number of other distractions.
- **You can't execute.** Constant disruptions make it impossible to manage your time and get things done. You're always running behind and playing catch-up, which leads to missed deadlines and mediocre work.

- **Forget about strategizing and planning. (It won't happen.)** Thriving organizations change, grow, and innovate. This requires time and space to think and plan ahead. You can't do it when there's no break from day-to-day chaos.

- **You are less mindful and more reactive.** Constant communication means less time and fewer opportunities to get present and centered. Without this grounding energy, you will have a harder time making thoughtful, conscious decisions. (You may even have temper flares and fly off the handle, which doesn't exactly help your relationships and career!)

- **You make careless (dare I say stupid?) mistakes.** Things begin to fall through the cracks. You're inconsistent and forgetful. You appear unprepared and scattered to those around you. You make bad decisions. You drop the ball often.

- **Your listening suffers . . .** Noise shrinks your attention span by filling your mind with useless information and jumbling your thoughts. You can't concentrate. It's hard to tune in to what others are saying.

- **. . . And clear communication goes out the window . . .** Without quiet time for thinking, you can't organize your thoughts. You can't do the groundwork needed to make your message tight and to the point. (If you've read my book *BRIEF: Make a Bigger Impact by Saying Less*, you know lean communication is a must in a world of shrinking attention spans!) So you ramble. You think out loud. You give instructions off the cuff.

- **. . . Which frustrates others, wastes their time, and keeps them from thriving.** When your instructions are vague and unfocused, you come across as indecisive or incompetent. Worse, you set employees up to fail. They don't understand what you need them to do, so they miss the mark. Their performance suffers. They come to dislike working with you.

- **Relationships are damaged (or never get developed in the first**

**place).** The communication habits I've just described will hardly help you win friends and influence people. But also, you won't have time or energy to foster *meaningful* connections and collaboration with fellow coworkers. Relationships that go beyond the surface require thoughtful conversations. In a noisy workplace, there's no time and space for those.

- **Your (mental) health takes a nosedive.** Constant connectivity, disruption, and distraction wears you down over time. Your stress levels rise; you become fatigued and suffer burnout. You might even become anxious or depressed. When you're not thriving at work, it's hard to thrive at all.

- **Finally, your personal life suffers.** After slogging through a workday of nonstop noise, you go home feeling spent. In this state of exhaustion, you can't fully inhabit your other roles. Family and friends pay the price. You are too wiped out to play with your kids or walk the dog. You and your partner pass like ships in the night. You see friends less often or not at all. Interests and personal development take a back seat to survival.

The soul-crushing conditions I've just described have been building for several decades. And as we'll discuss shortly, the sudden acceleration of generative AI has turned up the volume even higher. The blunt truth is your livelihood may be at risk. Even if it isn't, the volume of content that is beginning to be cranked out might bury you once and for all. AI is a game changer for sure—and if we don't learn to master this new level of noise, the outcome of that game is going to be disastrous.

## Quiet or Noise? It's Your Choice.

Ultimately, you'll need to decide if you want to be pulled down by noise's undertow ... or learn to master the current and swim forward.

Sure, you can keep doing what you've been doing. You can keep letting noise dominate your workplace (and your home life) and wonder why nothing ever changes:

- why you are more stressed, depleted, anxious, depressed, distracted, and more addicted to your devices than ever before
- why you struggle to think clearly, why your job leaves you full of stress and tension, and why you're not reaching your full potential
- why you wake up one day and notice that a good portion of your life has washed away in the deluge of screen time, pointless meetings, and mindless chatter

But I don't want you to maintain the noisy status quo. And I'm willing to bet that you don't want that, either.

You would rather learn why quiet works like nothing else to put you in control of your day, your career, and your very life. By the end of this book, you will know all you need to know to drastically improve the way you communicate, collaborate, work, and live.

## Getting Clear About What Quiet Means

Before we go any further, I want to explain what *quiet* means in the context of this book and in the context of a professional's workday. In general, when I mention quiet, I am referring to a specific time (or times) during the day when a person tunes out distractions in order to intentionally think, prepare, do deep work, innovate, rest, or reset (or enjoy a range of other solitary activities or pursuits that I will cover later). *Every* professional needs daily time and space for this level of focus and solitude, but we seldom get it unless we intentionally plan for it. Quiet is that intentional time alone with your thoughts. It is a practice that you will return to again and again, and eventually this simple habit will transform your work, your productivity, and even your life. Further, when leaders and employees collectively harness the power of quiet, an organization can perform like never before.

That said, at times in this book I will also mention *quiet* in a different context, as a general way of approaching various moments throughout the day. For example, there are many instances throughout a professional's day when being quiet—by which I mean literally refraining from speaking—can be greatly beneficial. For example, a well-timed pause during an important exchange of ideas or information can give you the needed time to breathe, think, and decide on an appropriate or beneficial response. (Generally, professionals don't take nearly enough of these quiet pauses; you will learn in the following pages how modern work culture encourages us to speak on the fly, resulting in a wealth of workplace problems!)

Learning to pause and be quiet during interactions with others is a highly useful tool for your toolbox. Among other situations, it can be beneficial when

- you are talking with others during meetings or impromptu chats;
- you are listening to someone speak and you'd like to share your opinion;
- you are leading a discussion or speaking in front of a group;
- someone asks you to do a task and you need to give them a response.

A daily *quiet practice* is linked to our ability to *be quiet* in circumstances such as these because it gives us the training to be able to pause instead of saying or doing the first thing that pops into our heads. Together, these uses of quiet have the potential to impact everything about the way we work and, ultimately, our careers.

Next, let us take a closer look at the way noise sickens workplaces . . . and, eventually, employees.

## BRIEFLY STATED

We are overwhelmingly steeped in noise, creating danger for individuals.

## QUIET CONSIDERATIONS

**DO I:** have too many things competing for my attention?

**WOULD I:** benefit from eliminating distractions?

**CAN I:** carve out times for quiet?

## Chapter 2

# The Workplace Is Sick (and We Are, Too)

We've just described the toll noise takes on humans. Well, since organizations are simply groups of humans who've agreed to come together for a common purpose, it stands to reason that the noise virus spreads and impacts everyone. The result is a company that cannot possibly be working at anything approaching full capacity.

Sure, many organizations appear healthy on the surface. But upon closer examination, you'll see that people from the top to the bottom of an organization are being ravaged, stressed, depleted, and crippled by noise.

The dysfunction often begins with the workplace culture. In many offices there's a palpable sense of urgency driven by the need for productivity and profit. That often manifests in a bias toward nonstop activity and the constant invitation to interact. The sharing of ideas is generally a good thing. But when there's no break from the collaboration and disruption, it can be toxic.

Open office concepts add to the chaos. (We'll delve into this problem later in chapter twenty.) There's little privacy, not enough space, too many distractions, and no escape from the constant chatter. That's hardly a recipe for productivity. In fact, nearly everything about the way we connect and communicate is harmful for organizations and employees.

**Scattered leaders set the tone.** Have you ever had a boss who seems to skip the thinking, reflecting, and strategizing parts of their job? They run, run, run, firing off orders before rushing to the next task. Their (vague and incomplete) instructions send employees down the wrong path. People miss the mark. If multiple leaders "lead" this way, the entire organization gets off track.

Meanwhile, scattered leadership gradually shifts the culture. Employees emulate the boss, either because they feel they must or because the boss's frenetic energy is contagious. Even if they crave a quieter work experience, there's no one to model a better way.

**Constant collaboration and communication are de rigueur.** Somehow, the corporate world seems to think *work* means constant availability for meetings, brainstorming sessions, and impromptu chats. Why else would so many companies force people to work out in the open or, at best, in cubicles that create a slight illusion of privacy? (Hello, loud personal caller next door!)

In a boundaryless world, people can invade your space at any moment. Further, you're expected to always be "on." Extroverts are revered, and the talents of introverts go overlooked. If you're not naturally a Chatty Cathy, you'd better be able to pass for one.

**We become thoughtless communicators . . .** We all constantly interact with one another, yet that interaction rarely drives us forward. There's far too much careless movement, undirected action, useless words, and pointless posturing.

Instead of pausing and thinking about what we want to convey and stating it clearly and concisely, we charge ahead. In the age of emails, texts,

Slack, cascading messages, and other communication modes, it's fast and easy to simply send another message. Our minds race, unable to process it all.

**... And thoughtless meeting holders.** We schedule too many meetings and brainstorming sessions, show up unprepared, wing it, and leave unenlightened. Too often, nothing concrete gets decided, and even if something does, it rarely gets acted on. Not only are all these meetings ineffective, as we'll discuss in the next chapter, but they may actually be harming us—both at work and on the home front!

**Finally, we succumb to this insanity and embrace it as normal.** Because noise is such a prominent feature of our modern world, we don't see it as threatening. Brilliant minds over the centuries have extolled the value of quiet (see chapter seven), but we must have lost the memo. We are so steeped in noise that we no longer hear it.

Music, podcasts, social media feeds, and YouTube videos have become the (relentless) soundtrack of our lives. Our smartphones send us alerts around the clock. We recover from one Teams meeting or Zoom call, spend a few minutes working, and—oops!—time for the next one! The research is staggering:

- We experience one interruption *every eight minutes*, or *six to seven interruptions per hour*. That equals fifty to sixty interruptions in an eight-hour workday.
- A task is not immediately returned to *40 percent* of the time following the interruption.
- Once interrupted by email or phone, workers do not get back to the prior task *50 percent* of the time.
- The estimated cost of interruptions to the American economy is *$650 billion per year!*[1]

We've collectively learned to proceed in spite of this noise, but we could be so much more productive at work and far healthier if we could find a way to lower the volume!

So ... by now it's clear that our workplaces have a bad case of noise sickness. You can see how easily and quickly this environment creates a self-destructive cycle. When you're overwhelmed by too much talking, collaboration, and distraction, you become more scattered, fatigued, and unfocused yourself. None of this is good for your mental health.

## It All Takes a Toll on Employee Well-Being

Let me break in for a moment and say: this book is not about wellness. It's a business book. I'm more concerned about performance, productivity, and profit margins than about helping people find their spiritual center or live a Zen life (and I suspect you are, too). However, it would be very bad business to ignore employee well-being.

Priorities have dramatically shifted in the past few years. Today's talent has certain expectations for their workplace experience. I won't go deeply into this subject (again, not the point of the book). What I will say, though, is that employees want leaders who view them as individuals and care about them. A big part of that is keeping a watchful eye on their psychological well-being. According to a Deloitte survey, 70 percent of professionals feel that employers aren't doing enough to prevent and alleviate burnout, and 21 percent say their company does not offer any program to help alleviate burnout.[2] Since workplace stress costs the US economy an average of $300 billion per year, leaders should recognize this employee concern.[3]

And leaders *are* taking notice. The COVID-19 pandemic put things in perspective for many employees, and the Great Resignation of 2021 showed us that more people are thinking about what they truly want out of work. One of their major wants is better leaders. A study by organizational consulting firm Korn Ferry shows that leadership is starting to take notice. The study shows that leaders of the best-run companies are displaying new qualities that are essential to building a more caring and empathetic workplace. It says that "showing interpersonal savvy and instilling trust—have become more important with the coronavirus placing employees under new physical and mental strains."[4] This is great news, but we can all go further to create workplaces where we want to be. This book will show you how.

Speaking of mental strains, COVID-19 brought the issue of mental health out of the shadows and empowered people to talk about this long-stigmatized topic. We've started having conversations around tough subjects like stress, anxiety, depression, and burnout. Employees expect (and deserve) employers who take these issues seriously and create conditions where they can thrive. And as the Great Resignation has shown us, people leave when their needs are not met.

It's not hard to see how exposure to too much noise at work can impact our mental health:

- **We chase our tails.** Instead of taking thoughtful action to advance our careers, we are always in reaction mode because the noise keeps us playing perpetual catch-up.
- **We lose (vital) human connections.** Humans are wired to connect, but noise makes it nearly impossible to do so at work. In lieu of conversations, we all talk *at* each other (and over each other) instead of *to* each other. This leaves us feeling empty and lonely.
- **We succumb to anxiety.** It's hard not to be anxious when we're plagued by constant interruptions. We know we're not focusing on the right things. We know we're wasting our time. We know deadlines are looming. Meanwhile, the pressure to produce work is incessant. This creates a never-ending cycle of stress and worry.

- **We drift aimlessly.** As noise drains our energy, our careers stagnate. We just get through the day instead of setting and reaching goals to help us get that promotion or to create projects we really want to work on.
- **We burn out.** We lose our love for our work and our pride in doing it well. It's no secret that unhappiness with our work impacts mental health. It puts us at risk for depression, anxiety, sleep problems, and more.

I could go on, but you get the picture: workplaces dominated by noise are bad for all of us. So if we know that the workplace is sick, why aren't we doing something about it?

One of the biggest reasons is this: quiet goes against our social norms. We've all bought into the notion that offices must be bustling with constant activity. All employees should be chatty, extroverted, and ready to collaborate at a moment's notice. If not, people must not be working hard enough, or there is something wrong with them.

In reality, people just don't work this way. Professionals who never have quiet grow fatigued and frazzled. They can't think, they can't produce, and their job satisfaction plummets. I don't want to work that way, and I bet you don't, either.

## Five Reasons Why You Don't Have Time to Think at Work

Deep thinking is a hard but critical part of any professional's job. It's a must-have for problem-solving, strategizing, and innovating. Yet thinking is woefully missing in the workplace. Quite simply, many employees are too busy working to have time to think. Here are a few reasons why:

1. **Most people start their day with technology.** Research shows some of our best thinking happens in the morning when we wake up. Yet most people sleep by their smartphone and instinctively grab it first thing. When we check our smartphone, we set the wrong tone for the day. It then becomes habitual for us to look to technology for insights and answers throughout the day. Not only is it a bad habit, but it also stresses our brain and inhibits our "free-flow thinking" that occurs when the brain is in the theta stage—the relaxed, meditative state of mind. In an *Inc.* article titled "How Einstein and Edison Solved Problems in Their Sleep,"[5] Kate Rodriguez argues that if we can avoid technology during this awakening cycle and not force our brains to jump to the more intense beta stage— the highest level of brain frequency—we can better "have a free flow of ideas about yesterday's events or to contemplate the activities of the forthcoming day. This time can be extremely productive and can be a period of very meaningful and creative mental activity."

2. **Our door is always open.** Professionals are too quick to collaborate and respond. Many of them mistakenly feel that they must be always on, always available. Whether that means they are open for the office drive-by or free online 24/7, they're training colleagues and clients to always come calling—and rarely say no when they do.

3. **We can't embrace the quiet.** There's a strong impulse to talk at work, whether it's in a meeting, on Zoom calls, or while checking in on teammates. For most people, being silent not only feels uncomfortable and unproductive but also doesn't look like real work. Deep work means setting boundaries and being alone with your thoughts.

4. **Everyone suffers from "productivity paranoia."** A recent Microsoft study reports that overlapping meetings (being double-booked) increased by 46 percent per person in 2021. During those meetings, 42 percent multitasked.[6] In a hybrid work environment, which many organizations now embrace, leaders fear employees are not working while those same professionals are spending more time at work, online and in meetings. In other words, showcasing your "doing" supersedes time to think.

5. **We aren't scheduling time to think.** Our lives at work are driven by calendars and appointments. Unfortunately, most professionals do not intentionally set aside time to think and treat it conscientiously as an appointment to read, analyze, prepare, and choose a course of action. Many simply get comfortable with mainly thinking on the fly.

Professionals need to put collaboration and concentration in balance with each other. Thinking drives communicating. Although noise is working against us, we must somehow find a way to think first, then act.

I promise I'm not trying to frighten or discourage you. Rather, I want to help you understand the far-reaching impact noise has on organizations and individuals. This book is full of solutions and strategies to help leaders and employees at all levels take back control, learn to tune out the noise, and start to create and protect the quiet you crave at a deep level.

No matter where you are right now, I have full faith that quiet can transform every element of your life and unlock the creativity, thoughtfulness, and achievement that so often can feel out of reach. Let's continue.

## BRIEFLY STATED

Noise hurts the workplace as a whole and adds to our growing fatigue.

## QUIET CONSIDERATIONS

**DO I**: struggle with constant interruptions during the workday?

**WOULD I**: like to hand in my superficial "badge of busyness" to do deeper work?

**CAN I**: challenge myself to find strategies to tune out the noise?

# Chapter 3

# TMI, TMC
# (Too Much Information,
# Too Much Collaboration)

Let's revisit our earlier analogy comparing the workplace to a hive of bees. These busy pollinators work together morning to night to reach common goals. They are also in constant communication, using dance to share the location of nectar nearby. Much like our bee buddies, we too try hard to be collaborative and productive. But—thankfully, since we depend on them for our very existence!—bees are *so* much better at it than we are!

The sad truth is most human collaboration is incredibly inefficient. That is, we do too much of it, and we (often) do it badly. There is so much wasted time, so many pointless meetings, so much useless information flying about. No one has time (or makes time) to think, prepare, and communicate thoughtfully. People tend to wing it, think out loud, and talk past each other. There may be some viable ideas flung about, but generally, not much of substance happens after that. (We've got the hive ... but where's the honey?)

We certainly can't blame a lack of tools for our lack of execution. We have email, Slack, Microsoft Teams, WebEx, Trello, and all their ilk to keep us connected. We have too many search engines, social media sites, and other digital platforms to even begin to name them all. Information has never been more abundant, more "in your face," more *relentless*.

So, when *do* we have time to think, to bring form and shape to the free-flowing mass of information, and to execute on the plans that come out of it?

We *don't* have the time . . . or the energy . . . or the wherewithal. We are in an age of TMI (too much information) and TMC (too much collaboration). Instead of tuning in to focus and create, we all tune out so we can survive. And until we force ourselves to stop (or at least pause) the merry-go-round and find some quiet corner where we can think, nothing will change.

## TMI and TMC Cost Us Dearly

Lest you think I'm exaggerating, let's see what the *Wall Street Journal* had to say in a 2023 article Ray Smith wrote on these topics.[1] Here are a few of the revelations:

**We are drowning in meetings and email.** Data collected from workers who use Microsoft's business applications showed that many professionals spend the equivalent of two workdays a week in meetings and on email.

The article continues: "Researchers found that the 25% most active users of its apps—in other words, people who use Microsoft's business software for much of their online work activity—spent an average of 8.8 hours a week reading and writing emails and 7.5 hours logging meetings.

"Those figures don't include time spent instant messaging, on the phone or in other, impromptu conversations with co-workers. In all, the average employee spent 57% of their time using office software for communication—in meetings, email, chat. The remainder of time, 43%, they used for creating things, such as building spreadsheets or writing presentations."

**No wonder we can't find time to do our "real" job!** A different study by Microsoft revealed that nearly two out of three people (from a survey of 31,000) "struggled to find time and energy to do their actual job. Those people were more than three times as likely as others polled to say innovation and strategic thinking were a challenge for them." Jared Spataro, who leads Microsoft's modern-work team and headed up the research, said, "People feel quite overwhelmed, a sense of feeling like they have two jobs, the job they were hired to do, but then they have this other job of communicating, coordinating, and collaborating."

**It's costing our companies big bucks.** The article continues: "In a 2022 Harris Poll survey of more than 1,200 workers and executives, bosses estimated that their teams lost an average 7.47 hours a week—nearly an entire day—to poor communications. Based on an average salary of $66,967, the lost time translates to a cost of $12,506 for an employee annually, according to the report conducted on behalf of Grammarly, a proofreading-software company."

TMI and TMC are ruining our lives and crippling our organizations. People are not machines. We simply aren't wired to always be "on." We need time to think quietly, work alone, and allow our minds to rest. *Only* by fulfilling our human needs will we be able to be the thoughtful humans that will survive the AI explosion.

I recall feeling overwhelmed and helpless from TMI and TMC when I was invited to speak at a large national sales conference. I had colleagues to support in numerous breakout sessions and dealt with nonstop days of working, collaborating, providing and receiving updates, and rehearsing. It was intense to the point where I felt I couldn't breathe, since there were no gaps in the schedule. No time for quiet. Knowing what I know now—and practice now—I should have scheduled pockets of time to plan and unwind and not let the schedule consume me: quiet appointments instead of jumping into unplanned collaboration. Quiet could have directed me to hone in on why I was there and to more clearly define my role and my value to the client and my colleagues. Our most important core values are easy to lose in these moments where we feel overwhelmed and feel we can't say no to the influx of information and the expectation of constant collaboration.

I'm not saying we can stop communicating and collaborating with our teams and coworkers altogether. We probably can't even throttle it back all that much. What we can do is approach it all in a different way. It's the quality—not the quantity—of these exchanges that makes the difference.

High-quality collaboration lets us connect on a deeper level. We can share the information that is important and then disband to do our portion of the work, project, or task. It opens up time and energy we otherwise would not have. A study conducted by Microsoft backs up this idea.

## Microsoft Study: Less Collaboration and More Focus Helps People Thrive

Like most organizations, Microsoft once strived to measure engagement as the benchmark for success and satisfied employees. But they continually found that, despite high engagement scores, employees were struggling. A 2022 article in the *Harvard Business Review* titled "Why Microsoft Measures Employee Thriving, Not Engagement"[2] shares how Microsoft's People Analytics team set out to explore this disconnect and then made a big discovery. What they found was that *thriving*, not engagement, is the key to employee happiness. (For the record, they define thriving as "to be *energized* and *empowered* to do *meaningful work*.")

They also learned that thriving at work is not the same thing as having work–life balance. That's an important distinction in our new era of hybrid and remote work, where the lines are sometimes blurred between our work and personal lives. To address this, the team started gathering data on thriving and work–life balance.

In doing so, they found some interesting insights:

> ...those with the best of both worlds had five fewer hours in their workweek span, five fewer collaboration hours, three more focus hours, and 17 fewer employees in their internal network size.

What this tells me is that these employees who are thriving and achieving work–life balance have more time in their day to focus and to think. They have fewer people interrupting them for collaboration and fewer people to deal with in general. In other words, more *quiet*.

The article continues:

> This reinforces what we know from earlier work-life balance research and network size analysis, which showed us that increased collaboration does have a negative impact on employees' perception of work-life balance. It also confirms that collaboration is not inherently bad—for many employees, those times of close teamwork and striving toward a common goal can fuel thriving. However, it is important to be mindful of how intense collaboration can impact work-life balance, and leaders and employees alike should guard against that intensity becoming 24/7.

There you have it. Reducing collaboration is key for thriving *and* work–life balance. It empowers employees to take the quiet that they desperately need. They can think, reflect, read, work, and choose to be inaccessible when it matters most.

## Collaboration Overkill ... And What to Do About It

Remember that collaboration isn't inherently bad. But neither is constant collaboration good or beneficial. Some tasks, projects, and endeavors simply don't need to be done "by committee." We should trust our employees, our teammates, and ourselves to work well independently and to reach out if necessary. Otherwise, we risk them (and us) burning out. A good rule of thumb to follow is: better collaboration is *less* collaboration.

In a *Harvard Business Review* article titled "Where We Go Wrong with Collaboration," Babson College professor Rob Cross observes that we often overdo collaboration in the workplace. He shares that even before the COVID-19 pandemic, people spent "85% or more of their time each week in collaborative work—answering emails, instant messaging, in meetings, and using other team collaboration tools and spaces."[3] Since then, that number has increased. (Who could forget the Zoom fatigue of 2020?)

But not everyone is struggling. Cross reveals that while nearly everything we do in a professional setting is some sort of collaboration, the people who are performing at the top of their game and thriving in their work collaborate 18 to 24 percent more efficiently than their peers.

Interviews with these top performers revealed the three behaviors that made them better collaborators:

1. They identify challenging beliefs that lead us to collaborate too quickly.
2. They impose structure in their work to prevent unproductive collaboration.
3. They alter behaviors to create more efficient collaboration.

Cross revealed that 50 percent or more of the problem of collaborative overload stems from those pesky challenging beliefs we have about ourselves mentioned in behavior number one. These are the "deeply held, and often unexamined desires, needs, expectations and fears centered around how we feel we need to 'show up' for others each day." Cross explored some of these typical internal triggers that professionals might need to become aware of and/or guard against to prevent collaborative overload. For brevity, I will paraphrase them here in my own words:

- I want to help others, so I say yes all the time (or too often).
- I love the rush of accomplishment, so I seek more and more collaboration.
- I'm an information magnet. I need to know it all.
- I'm worried that I'm not good enough, so I ask to be abused with too much information.
- My desire for perfection leads to constant communication.
- I'm needed for everything, so I need to know everything.
- Everything starts with, ends with, and circles back to me.
- The plan must be picture perfect and clear, and I'll go deep into the weeds to get there.
- I need to know all there is to know, and you must tell me everything.

> To learn more, check out the *Just Saying* podcast, episode "HBR Article Review: Overcoming Collaboration Overkill": podcast.thebrieflab.com/ep-247-hbr-article-review-overcoming -collaboration-overkill.

Most of us recognize ourselves in at least some of these statements. I certainly do and reflect on a time when a colleague shared that collaboration isn't necessarily a time for thinking. He challenged me to "think alone; plan collaboratively." Since collaborating and thinking are two different tasks, we need to think on our own—then go to our collaboration time with more thoughtful ideas in order to plan, prepare, perfect, and decide.

What will make a difference is learning to challenge these beliefs. The next time you have a knee-jerk reaction, take a pause to consider whether you really need to be involved. You always have the power to say, "No, not now," and protect your time and space for quiet.

Even still, there are times when collaboration is necessary. Professionals need to work together a certain amount to set and achieve their goals and innovate for the future. But in those moments, a more mindful and targeted approach is best. I recommend that professionals follow the principles used by my company, The BRIEF Lab, in its mission to help organizations and individuals master concise communication and improve operational efficiency and effectiveness. Further, these principles embody the remaining two behaviors of the top performers mentioned in the *Harvard Business Review* article above, as they actively prevent unproductive collaboration and create more efficient collaboration. They are:

- **Less is more.** Trim the information you share with others. When in doubt, stick to what you feel people will really care about.
- **Be more intentional.** Think before you speak or write to others. Don't speak off the cuff or wing it when communicating. Take more quiet time to prepare.
- **Reduce habitual collaboration.** Cancel (or stop scheduling) needless meetings. But when you do need to meet, schedule only the amount of time you need to cover the information on the carefully crafted agenda.
- **Spend more time alone.** If you have the option to work independently in quiet, do it! (Remember, you can always converge again to discuss, analyze, and fine-tune your individual work.)

I believe that when we make the effort, we can find a happy medium between working together and working alone in quiet. We can value collaboration while appreciating that we must also prioritize time for focus and concentration. We can learn to say no to the overabundance of information flowing through most organizations.

Achieving a balance (or something close to it) between these opposing tensions is possible when *we* get to decide when we need to put our heads together with others and when we need to retreat to our own space (and headspace). Success is even more likely when we learn the skills and tools that I'll cover later in the book to help you mitigate the noise and build a haven of quiet.

But first, let's look at the important role of leaders in setting the tone for everyone else.

## BRIEFLY STATED

There is an abundance of inefficient collaboration in most workplaces, so we need more quiet time to make it more effective.

## QUIET CONSIDERATIONS

**DO I:** feel frustrated with increasing information, meetings, and collaborations that limit the time I have to do my actual job?

**WOULD I:** like to thrive and be empowered to do deeper, more meaningful work?

**CAN I:** eliminate unnecessary collaboration to increase opportunities to focus and think?

## Chapter 4

# Thoughtless, Scattered Leaders Scare Us

E ven if we haven't been lucky enough to work for a great leader, we know what they *should* be like. Don't we? Great leaders think before they speak and act. They are intentional in their planning and decision-making. Being thoughtful and deliberate also makes them good communicators. They are clear with their messages and can explain the reasons behind their decisions and requests. It's not an accident that great leaders have these qualities. They know that doing their job well means putting in the hard (quiet) work up front.

*Great leaders protect their time to think and strategize.*

They deliberately build it into their routines. Allotting this time takes careful (and consistent) planning. It means closing the door, blocking out distractions, and doing the hard work of thinking. Quite often, it means telling others no.

We love methodical leaders who think before speaking and acting because they help us know exactly what we're supposed to do. There's little to no ambiguity. We don't often have to scrutinize their instructions, second-guess ourselves, or go back to them with a thousand questions before we can move ahead. These leaders are consistent in both their instructions and their expectations. Working for them is like a breath of fresh air.

On the other hand ...

> **Scattered leaders think too much on the fly. (And spin in all directions like a weather vane.)**

No one wants to work for a thoughtless, erratic, scattered leader. It's exhausting. These leaders are chaotic. They are inconsistent and unpredictable. They jump from one initiative to the next, forcing employees to constantly reprioritize and change direction. It's impossible to guess where this kind of leader is going. Most likely, *they* don't even know.

Despite their lack of direction, scattered leaders are *constantly* moving. They are all action with little to no thought behind the activity. Many of them don't even realize this is a problem. That's because we put busy people up on a pedestal. We aspire to become that person who is always on the go, who has lots of irons in the fire, and who has an overbooked calendar. It's almost a rite of passage: once we're so busy that we can hardly think straight, we believe we have "arrived."

I have had my own run-ins with scattered leaders. I once worked with a person who reminded me of a pendulum. From one day to the next, their attitude and direction would change. They were up; they were down. One day everything was great. The next day everything was terrible. I could never gauge the state of our projects because they would swing from one extreme to the other. It was a mental and emotional roller coaster. I'd start in one direction, then get yanked in another. My hard work would get tossed. It was tedious to work with this person, and we all had little to no confidence in their leadership.

When I titled this chapter, I wasn't exaggerating. Working for scattered leaders *is* scary. They keep you disoriented, off-balance, and anxious about what's coming next. Each new project—heck, each new day—is accompanied by a gnawing sense of dread.

No one should have to work this way or for someone like this.

## Thoughtless Leaders Ruin Employees' Chances for Success...

If you're an employee, working for a scattered leader is bad for your career. If they're your client, you hate them and your job. Even if you desperately want to do a good job (and I believe most people do), you can't. You have to spend too much time wading through too much information and asking questions. You have to backtrack or change directions on the leader's whims. You have to invent workarounds.

It's not fair, but all of this makes *you,* the employee or business provider, look scattered and thoughtless as well. You end up in the career slow lane.

## ... They Cripple Organizations ...

It's pretty obvious that spending day after day being unable to execute is a morale killer. Good employees don't want to be told one thing on Monday only to be told something completely different on Tuesday. They want clear, consistent leaders who empower them to excel.

Some of these talented employees will say enough is enough. They might put up with a bad leader for a while, but eventually, they'll get antsy and leave. Really, who can blame them?

Others will hang in there, but they'll stop trying. For whatever reason—low confidence, scarcity thinking, or plain old lack of gumption—they'll resign themselves to a work life of quiet desperation. Their performance will drop to "just getting by" level. Rather than putting the full force of their creativity and brainpower to work, they'll do the minimum amount of work possible.

What's left is a dysfunctional workforce—the opposite of the power-house team needed to compete in today's hypercompetitive economy.

## ... And They're Not Doing Themselves Any Favors, Either

Most leaders are judged by their results. If you're a scattered leader, the truth is you're probably not getting them. You might hold on to your job in an organization that tolerates mediocrity, but you won't be on the promotion list. Headhunters won't beat down your door. And if personal fulfillment means anything to you—well, sorry, you're not going to enjoy a lot of that, either.

Now you might be thinking, *Joe, of course I'm not* choosing *to be a scattered, thoughtless leader!* I know that. Most leaders have good intentions. They are aware, underneath the noise and chaos and constant activity, that there has to be a better way. But—like everyone else—they're products of a sick workplace.

## Why Are There So Many Scattered, Thoughtless Leaders?

If you've read this far, none of this will come as a surprise. Today's leaders have a lot of habits, factors, and traits—many relating to noise—working against them. For example ...

**Competing priorities.** It's common for leaders to have several different bosses, each with their own priorities and agendas. Keeping them all happy with your work is a full-time job in itself.

**Distractions galore.** There are a million people calling, texting, emailing, and Slacking you all the time. And the higher up you are, the more interruptions you may have:

- **Nearly 50 percent** of executives are interrupted **five to ten times** during a typical business day. **Twenty-nine percent** are interrupted **two to three times** every hour.
- **Thirty-five percent** of executives say that an **interruption** lasts for **three to five minutes,** and 21 percent say **five or more.**[1]

**Always being "on."** Many leaders make themselves available 24/7 (it's practically required now that remote work has further blurred our work–life boundaries). This means you're even less likely to make room for quiet in your busy life.

**Stress (at work and at home).** Like everyone else, leaders have demands and stressors from their private life. It's hard to leave all that at the door when you go to work.

**Trouble saying no.** You want to do a great job and you want to please people, so you overcommit and take on more than you can handle.

**Internal noise.** You are at the mercy of your brain and its many thoughts. It's noisy, anxious, and crowded in there!

Existing in a state of scatter means you're constantly being pulled in all directions at once. Your brain can't grab on to what's most important, so your attention remains divided and your work and relationships continue to suffer.

Not good. Not fun.

The good news is you can mend your scattered ways! The advice in later portions of this book will help you fundamentally shift the way you live, work, and lead. We'll take a deep dive into daily practices, habit shifts, and methods that will help you prioritize thinking and build more quiet into your life. But for now, here's some advice to think about as you continue reading.

## How to *Internally* Limit Scattered Leadership

Becoming a thoughtful leader starts by addressing your inner world. Once you're more easily able to pause, lean into the quiet, and hear yourself think, it is easier to do the planning and strategizing that leaders must do. A few tips:

**Make room for quiet time,** *no matter what.* Schedule it every day as a nonnegotiable appointment. This is a commitment you must make for yourself. No one else will hold you to it, so it's up to you to make it happen.

You don't need to complicate your quiet. In fact, you should be willing to do it poorly. All you need is five or ten minutes to put away all technology and do the thinking, reading, planning, deciding, or any other quiet-oriented task that you need to do in that moment. Not only does this refresh your mind and body, but it also enables the *brain* itself to work better, says Samantha Artherholt, a psychologist and clinical associate professor in the University of Washington School of Medicine's Department of Rehabilitation. She explains, "What we're learning is some of the same consolidation activities that happen in our brains when we're asleep also occur when we rest." In other words, "allowing yourself [downtime] with minimal stimuli helps replenish your brain's capacity for attention, focus, and creativity, and it allows you to process new information you've learned and tie it to other ideas."[2]

Be sure to schedule the time for quiet, though. This should be an appointment that you keep the same way you would any other professional obligation. Put it in your planner or program it into your calendar. And stick with it no matter what.

**Weigh your competing priorities.** Put pen to paper and list them all out. (You can do this exercise as part of your quiet time!) Once you've got them all in front of you, do some reflecting. Which are most important? Do some create more stress and confusion than others? What do you need to focus on first, second, and so on?

It's important to take time to think about everything that is expected of you instead of rushing through each day. When you can answer questions like *What's the best thing that happened today? The worst thing? What do I really need to do today? What is less important?* you will have a lot more mental space to focus on what matters most.

## How to *Externally* Manage Scattered Leadership

Once quiet has improved your inner world, it's time to test-drive your communication and other external leadership roles. Here are a few steps to get you started:

**Make "Think, Speak, Do" your new mantra.** Thinking should *always* precede speaking. Thinking should *always* precede doing. If you speak or do anything without first thinking, well, that makes you a thoughtless professional. This important "order of operations" is surprisingly missing in the routines of many executives . . . and it certainly shows!

When I say *think*, I am referring to giving yourself time for quiet. You can use quiet for things other than thinking, of course, but often you will find during quiet times that your mind wanders to a question that needs answering or a problem that needs solving. So I am using *thinking* as our catchall verb for whatever you choose to fill your quiet with.

You will become more intentional, effective, and influential by putting the key ingredient—thinking—at the beginning of the sequence where it belongs. This is one of the most important takeaways I want you to gain from this book: *Think. Speak. Do.* By the way, this is true for all employees, no matter their title, but it's absolutely imperative for anyone who leads others.

I use this mantra when prepping for meetings, projects, or updates. In many organizations, when you do meeting planning, you are given a set of expectations and directions to follow. But if you take time to think first of the amount of time you need for preparation and consider your agenda, your role in the meeting, and the participants' roles, and then establish a minimum definition of success by the end of the meeting, you will set yourself up for success. The higher the ratio of *thinking* before you actually *speak* and *do*, the lower the amount of time you'll spend aimlessly talking at the meeting, searching for an agenda. A lower ratio of thought to action means too much talking. Good preparation drives a well-thought-out agenda, which leads to clear action steps. It creates a cycle where the leader can then reflect upon questions like "Did we execute?" and "What did we do right or wrong?" Think, Speak, Do has a prolific impact when we do it well. But if we don't, it's like the definition of insanity—doing the same thing over and over and expecting a different outcome.

Putting Think, Speak, Do into practice is simple once you commit to it. For example, before you go into a meeting, take some time to think about what you want to share with or convey to others. You will know ahead of time how you feel about the topics you want to discuss, and you won't be thinking as words are coming out of your mouth. Notice how this helps you achieve more impactful communication.

For a deeper dive into Think, Speak, Do, listen to the *Just Saying* podcast, episode "Avoid 'Trouble' as a Thinker, Talker, and Doer," where we'll explore one of my favorite Coldplay songs and learn to avoid the web of confusion caused by noise: podcast.thebrieflab .com/ep-296-avoid-trouble-as-a-thinker-talker-and-doer.

**Be brief, be clear, be concise.** In a world of way too much information, it is a gift to be brief. I cover this topic extensively in my book *BRIEF: Make a Bigger Impact by Saying Less*, so if you want a deep dive into the art of lean communication, give it a read. But for now, start practicing communicating your messages to employees, colleagues, and other leaders using only the essential details. Be clear. Don't complicate things with unnecessary information.

My rule to help you keep your messaging simple and clear: If you don't have to say it, don't say it. If you do have to say it, say it. Eliminate wasteful words and you will do yourself and your colleagues a favor. Plus, you'll set yourself apart.

**Communicate for the benefit of others.** Leaders, remember who you are communicating for. (Hint: it's not about you.) What you say and write is for the benefit of others: your team, your colleagues, or your own bosses. But when every word coming out of your mouth happens on the fly—with no forethought—it's likely that you will negatively impact the very people that rely on your direction and guidance. If you're all over the place, they will be, too.

To learn more, check out the *Just Saying* podcast, episode "Scattered": podcast.thebrieflab.com/ep-210-scattered.

These changes are just the beginning of the journey that will make you a better, more focused, and clearer communicator and leader. They are small but mighty ways to lower the noise for yourself, which in turn lowers the noise for those around you. And with the recent rapid emergence of artificial intelligence making our noisy workplace even noisier, you can't afford to ramble or give too much information. Next up, we'll look at the new world of generative AI and what all professionals should know to get ready.

## BRIEFLY STATED

The gap between scattered leaders and effective leaders lies in the planning. Great leaders take time to think and plan before communicating, while scattered leaders continue to spin out of control.

## QUIET CONSIDERATIONS

**DO I:** plan out deliberate and intentional communication before engaging my audience?

**WOULD I:** benefit from an "internal audit" to learn how to prioritize opportunities for quiet in my workday routine?

**CAN I:** implement the practice of Think, Speak, Do in my spoken and written interactions?

# Chapter 5

# AI Is Making Things
# a Lot Worse

As if our "perfect storm" of noise-fueled distraction, diversion, and disruption wasn't enough to deal with, new developments in artificial intelligence just disrupted the status quo. And it will continue to make everything *so much worse.*

Generative AI is changing the world as we know it. Machine learning has enabled natural language processing tools like OpenAI's ChatGPT and Google's Bard to generate new data, images, audio, video, and text that imitate human-created content. With a few keystrokes, we now have infinite and immediate ways to create and communicate.

This is both super exciting and a little frightening. Where you land on the spectrum depends on whether your gut reaction is "Wow, this will help me do my job even better!" or "Oh no! This is going to steal my job!" Turns out, a lot of people fall somewhere in the middle. A recent survey from the Pew Research Center finds that many US workers in more exposed industries do not feel their jobs are at risk. For instance, 32 percent of workers in information and technology say AI will help more than hurt them personally. (Only 11 percent say it will hurt more than it helps.)[1] Yet, according to a recent report by economists Daron Acemoglu at MIT and Pascual Restrepo at Boston University, robots could replace two million employees in manufacturing alone by 2025.[2]

No matter how you feel AI will impact your life and career, one thing is clear: the massive wave of content has made our noisy world of work, well, *a lot noisier*. If you think our culture that normalizes TMI and TMC is painful now, just wait until AI is adding to the cacophony full force.

Today there's more information than ever before that we must wade through, process, and use (or discard). A year from now, there will be even more. While we don't yet know the full impact AI will have on our world, we do know that in a short period of time, droves of people have embraced generative AI technology.

Salesforce's ongoing Generative AI Snapshot Research Series reveals who is currently using AI and how they are using it. They shared the following insights:

- Forty-five percent of the US population surveyed is using generative AI.
- Seventy-five percent of generative AI users are looking to automate tasks at work and use generative AI for work.
- Sixty-five percent of generative AI users are millennials or Gen Z, and 72 percent are employed.
- Of the five hundred IT professionals surveyed, 67 percent said they have prioritized generative AI for their business within the next eighteen months.
- Of the over one thousand marketers surveyed, 51 percent are already using or are experimenting with generative AI at work—and 22 percent report that they plan to use it soon. The most common uses of generative AI among marketers are basic content creation (76 percent), writing copy (76 percent), and inspiring their critical thinking (71 percent).

- Seven in ten marketers (71 percent) expect generative AI to help eliminate busywork and allow them to focus more on strategic work.[3]

If you don't know how to capture some quiet for yourself, you will never be able to determine what is important and what is just meaningless noise.

Let's take a closer look at artificial intelligence and what it means for us.

## The Basics of Generative AI

Chances are, you've already heard a lot about AI. Perhaps you even use it in your personal or professional life. But in case you need some background, here's a quick primer: generative AI refers to a type of artificial intelligence that can create new content, such as images, music, text, or videos, that is similar to or inspired by existing data. Generative models use deep learning techniques, such as neural networks, to generate new examples by learning patterns from large amounts of training data. Generative AI can be used in a variety of applications, such as art, music, and video creation, content generation for social media, language translation, chatbots, and even gaming.

As a word guy, I was naturally drawn to ChatGPT. When I started playing around with it, I was blown away by all it can do. For example, I gave it a command to write a poem about the threats of generative AI. The first stanza of the six-stanza poem it delivered a moment later read:

*The rise of machines, a modern threat,*
*A force of nature we can't forget,*
*Artificial intelligence, so clever,*
*May one day turn on us, forever.*

Chilling, and accurate.

Then I asked it to summarize, in twenty words, the Gettysburg Address. Boom. The response was brief, clear, eloquent. I revised the command, asking for a forty-word summary. It didn't disappoint.

The more I experimented with this technology, the more amazed I became. I started to realize that we now have a tool that is remarkably accurate, that generates content quickly, that can seamlessly assist us with research and everyday tasks ... and so much more.

But looking at generative AI in the context of this book, my biggest concern isn't what it does—it's the speed at which it does it. That's the real disruptor.

*AI is like a bullet train speeding by us. And we're on a bicycle.*

This technology works so much faster than our human brains could ever hope to. In mere seconds we can generate content, do research, or get help with tedious tasks that once robbed us of our time and energy. It's exciting but (as I mentioned earlier) also threatening. The truth is, AI is so fast and efficient that we will never be able to compete with some of what it does.

So where does that leave us?

I, for one, am cautiously optimistic. I don't believe this technology is going to take all our jobs (as I'll describe below, it can't replicate the things we do that are uniquely human—at least not yet). I do believe it gives us humans a unique opportunity. But to make the most of it, we need to understand and embrace the things AI *can* do for us.

For example, here are a few ways generative AI can optimize your work and improve your communication.

**It is a powerful content creator for verbal and written communication.**
Anyone who writes, speaks, or otherwise communicates for a living—and

whether you think of yourself this way or not, as a leader that's what you do!—now has a partner and researcher like no other. You can treat many AI chatbots as you would a reference expert in your local library.

**It gives you a starting point for writing and communication.** I'm not suggesting you let ChatGPT do *all* the writing. But it *can* provide you with a great starting point by offering up a thought or perspective as a jumping-off point. Then you can edit and shape the text based on your knowledge of the audience—their unique circumstances, personal preferences, and other nuances that a computer can't possibly know.

**It jump-starts the creative process.** Who hasn't gotten stuck when trying to write? AI can help get the creative juices flowing. With a few commands you can discover perspectives that spark your creativity and light up your imagination. Examples might be a list of creative ways to promote a product or prompting it to write a draft of a poem, letter, or song that you can revise.

**It's a powerful research tool.** It's easy to fall down a rabbit hole when doing research. Chatbots can accelerate the process. You might ask, "What's the difference between calm and quiet?" and immediately get back a bulleted list. Or you can ask it to break down the most important characters in *Othello*. The results can quickly broaden your understanding of your topic.

**It's great for headlining**. Even when we've got a handle on the content, we may struggle to headline our work. That's too bad because headlining is the best way to get your message across quickly, whether you're creating a presentation or an email. I use the handy acronym BLUF—"bottom line up front"—when working on headlines. But headlining can be challenging at times for many writers. Chatbots can help you be clear and specific and grab the attention of the reader.

**It can be helpful for planning, strategy, and how-tos.** If you are looking to craft a plan, rework a strategy, or fix something, a few questions can prompt a list of initial recommendations to build upon. For example, AI can help you with launching a new product, addressing an unhappy customer, or setting boundaries between home and work.

> To learn more, check out the *Just Saying* podcast, episode "A Brief Take on AI and Communication (Part 1)": podcast.thebrieflab.com/ep-283-a-brief-take-on-a-i-and-communication-part-1.
>
> Also check out the *Just Saying* podcast, episode "A Brief Take on AI and Communication (Part 2)": podcast.thebrieflab.com/ep-284-a-brief-take-on-ai-communication-part-2.

As I continue experimenting with chatbots, I'm having far more "wow" moments than "oh no" moments. I think you will, too. Give them a try for researching, sparking ideas, and creating content, and see if they help you get your thoughts across any more easily.

## Exciting Takeaways and Bold Predictions: The New Frontier of AI

Drat, I seem to have misplaced my crystal ball (again)! But even so, here are some takeaways and predictions I feel comfortable making based on what I know about AI, lean communication, noise, and the future of work. You'll notice some of these are negative. But others show AI's potential to make us better communicators and help us fine-tune our work.

Here's a forecast of our future, as I see it.

**First, we will have even less time for quiet than before.** As content explodes, there will be an endless supply of information to digest. But, like always, we have no time to consume it. This worries me the most.

**There will be an instant content bonanza.** Everyone will become a good (not great, mind you) writer overnight. Professionals, content creators, influencers, bloggers, and others will start cranking out unprecedented amounts of content.

**Writing will lose its value.** As I mentioned, content quality will initially improve as more people utilize AI to do the initial writing. Yet the impact of AI-generated writing will quickly "go beige" as it all starts to sound monotonously similar (insert the "voice" of Charlie Brown's teacher here) and, eventually, fade. At some point the value of fresh, creative, *human*-generated writing will start to rise again. It will be easy for some people to abdicate their duty and let AI carry the load.

**Brevity will be more important than ever.** Clear, concise communication becomes nonnegotiable. No one has time for anything else. Be brief, be brilliant ... or be gone.

**Audio and video will keep eroding our trust.** In one of the dark sides of AI, deepfakes will continue cropping up, undermining our faith in digital media.

**In-person communication will take center stage.** As we flounder about in a sea of ho-hum writing and fake content, we will once again crave the connection of face-to-face interactions. If we can't trust AI, who can we trust? Humans, that's who.

**Personality will matter more and more.** Being authentic—and trust-worthy—makes you stand out. We will become freer to be our true selves and will be rewarded for it.

And finally, here's my biggest takeaway of all:

*Quiet* **will** *be the cornerstone of all we do.*

No doubt about it: natural language processing tools like ChatGPT and the like have already had and will continue to have far-reaching effects on our lives and work. These chatbots can do things we can't. The train has been set in motion, it's zipping down the track, and we shouldn't even try to outrun it. What we can do is stop, breathe, regroup, think . . . and sit serenely as the train thunders on by.

Don't get me wrong. This is not a "surrender, Dorothy" moment. I'm not asking you to stop doing your work and fade off into obsolescence. I'm asking you to do the opposite: get focused, sharp, smart, and determined. And I'm saying that means being quiet. Every day.

We *must* have quiet to formulate and communicate our thoughts and ideas. Doing that in a world that includes AI means asking the right questions so your partnership with these tools is effective—because there are now infinite answers at your fingertips. Quiet allows and empowers us to do the imperative thinking up front. Without this kind of thinking, we get lost in the noisy abyss.

The irony is the faster AI changes our lives, the more value we will gain by slowing down.

This technology has, indeed, cursed us with too many choices. (That's arguably as bad as too few!) But quiet helps make sense of those choices. It gives us the time and space to ask ourselves the questions we need to get clear on what we have to convey. Questions like: "Why is this important?" and "How will it really affect us?" and "So what?" and "What next?"

Quiet helps us consider our options, alternatives, implications, and recommendations. It's what allows us to make smarter decisions. It's the one element we can't live without as AI barrels relentlessly into our workplaces, lives, and futures.

## The Role of Quiet Query: Asking Better Questions Before You Chat

If you want to get the most out of your experience using chatbots, you've got to master the art of better prompting and asking more refined questions. You can't do it on the spot. Language processing tools are incredibly powerful, and they can unleash a world of knowledge—but only when you do the thinking and preparation up front.

Before we talk strategy, I want to emphasize that it's important to treat AI prompting like a real-life conversation with the smartest person on earth. The most breathtaking results I have generated have occurred when I act as if I'm having a conversation with Steve Jobs, or Bill Gates, or Stephen Hawking, or Elon Musk. I wouldn't dare show up to a conversation with one of these great thinkers (or with anyone, for that matter) without first preparing great questions.

Great questions matter. They're the key that can open up what you might learn from somebody. If you ask a terrible question—"How was your day?" or "What's up?"—the answer you receive will barely scratch the surface, and you won't learn anything substantive. Even "good" questions can end up giving you subpar results. But by giving the right prompts or asking great questions, you'll get back so much more than you can even imagine.

Just to hammer home the stark contrast of good versus great questions, see these examples:

- Instead of asking, "What exercises help you lose weight?" ask, "Tell me about exercises I can do to reduce stomach fat."
- Instead of prompting, "Write a catchy caption for my Instagram," try "Write a sarcastic caption about the stress of traveling in Italy."

So the question is: How do we ask great questions to get the results we want?

*Enter the quiet query.*

A quiet query is simply a thoughtful, intentional moment where you can formulate a better question. Quiet queries aren't just for AI prompts—they're for anyone we communicate with, from our family and friends to colleagues and team members.

But when it comes to using language processing tools like ChatGPT, quiet is more important than ever. Chatting without first having quiet is like jumping in the driver's seat of a high-performance sports car like a McLaren or Lamborghini with no forethought or preparation. Without understanding the power of those engines, you're not going to have the driving experience you hoped for—you'll just keep hitting the pedal and jerking the wheel.

You'll need time and silence to make use of the tools associated with chatbots that can optimize your results. There are endless ways to modify your prompts to craft content for any number of audiences. Here are a few prompting samples to give you an idea of what's possible:

Prompt Example 1: *Acting as a CEO, please write an analysis of the current state of the commercial real estate industry in the Pacific Northwest and its potential for investors. Show as presentation slides.*

Prompt Example 2: *Acting as a therapist, create a blog post on OCD behavioral therapy for teenagers. Write in professional and straightforward style.*

Here are four tips for forming a quiet query. This will serve you well as you partner with AI technology, but it will also make you a far stronger communicator in all of your relationships:

1. **Make time for quiet.** Schedule time to be alone with your thoughts prior to sitting down at your computer to work with a chatbot. Ask yourself things like: What am I looking for? What do I want to know? What am I interested in? Why am I curious? Where do I need clarification or better understanding?

2. **Write down your thoughts.** Go old school and grab a pencil and paper and jot down your thoughts surrounding the answers you seek. This will help you formulate the right prompts or questions. To organize your thoughts, use the acronym BRIEF:

   - Background: What's the current situation, issue, or problem?
   - Relevance: What do I want my audience to do with this information? What does this mean to my audience?
   - Information: What key pieces of information or ideas do I need to share to give my audience a clearer understanding of the situation?
   - Ending: How do I want to conclude? What does success look like?
   - Follow-up: What questions do I anticipate at the end? What questions should I ask to get my audience talking?

**If you would like to take a deeper dive into your preparations and queries, visit thebrieflab.com to download a BRIEF Map, a visual outline you can use in your prep work.**

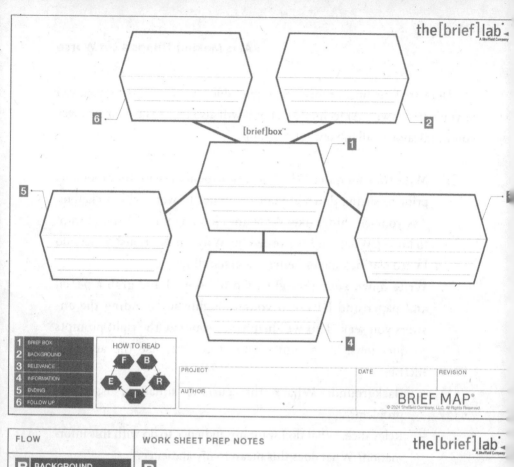

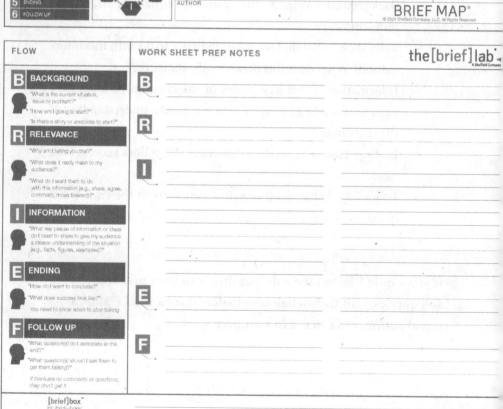

3.   **Take a cue from little kids and ask "Why?"** The question "Why?" is one of the most powerful questions in existence. Anyone who has spent time around a four- or five-year-old child can confirm that "Why?" is their favorite query. That's no coincidence. Even our youngest fellow humans possess our innate desire to dig deeper. As you are forming your quiet query, keep coming back to "Why?" "Why do I feel this way?" "Why does this matter?" Why is this a problem?" Asking "Why?" will guide you toward the message you want to create and convey.

4.   **Practice, practice, practice!** Most people struggle with asking open-ended questions. Instead, we ask simple questions that require one- or two-word answers and don't foster deeper communication. But this is a skill that can be developed with enough practice. So keep tinkering and experimenting, both in your AI prompting as well as in your daily life. Instead of asking, "How was your day?" you might ask, "What were the highs and lows of your day?" Instead of asking, "How was your trip?" you might ask, "How did you feel about your trip overall?" and then, "Is there anything you would do differently the next time?" When you're working with a chatbot, practice asking prompts to get familiar with what AI can do. Over time you will start asking better questions and getting the information you seek.

Remember, most people are not going to be naturally good at asking the right questions—whether virtually or face-to-face with real people. The quiet query is your time to workshop your skills and abilities in this area. It will take time—and silence—to really build your efficacy. But the payoff is huge and 100 percent worth it.

## AI Can Take Over the "Easy" Tasks That Steal Your Time

A 2023 article in the *Wall Street Journal* highlights the way organizations are starting to use AI features to lighten workloads. It shares that "Microsoft, which holds a large stake in OpenAI, the startup behind ChatGPT, is baking generative AI features into core workplace tools such as Outlook and PowerPoint to remove what its leaders have called the 'drudgery' of some work tasks. A majority of workers surveyed by the company said they think AI would help lessen their workloads, although nearly half said they worry the technology could imperil their job security."[4]

This is great news for harried workers everywhere—and the statistics from Salesforce earlier in this chapter indicate that professionals are already taking advantage of AI. Most professionals don't have the time or energy to waste doing these kinds of menial but necessary tasks. Now, thanks to automation, they will no longer have to. But as more organizations use AI to free up pockets of time, they must also build in a culture that values quiet. The reason? Because noise will always find a way to fill any void. If we don't prioritize quiet time that allows employees to focus, think, problem-solve, and execute, those hard-earned gains will be lost time and time again.

## Don't Worry: AI Will Not (And Cannot) Replace What Is Uniquely Human

Let's all take a deep breath and remember that we aren't doomed now that this technology exists. Humans invented it. Why *wouldn't* humans ultimately use it in a way that benefits us, not harms us? That's not to say there won't be a lot of disruption in the process, but that's okay. We're used to disruption, aren't we?

For now, let's think of AI as a supremely useful tool rather than as a weapon signaling our destruction. Anyone who uses communication (and that's pretty much folks in every profession I can think of!) can make the most of what AI offers us as thinkers, communicators, and leaders.

Yes, AI can do some things "better" than humans can. But there are still many uniquely human skills and abilities that AI can't touch:

- **Critical thinking and insights.** Chatbots can generate infinite information, but you are the one who gets to read it, comprehend it, and consider the implications. You will ask important questions like "So what?" and "Now what?" You might even criticize what you learn: Is it true? Is it viable?
- **Creativity and query.** You formulate the questions and prompts that will spark your creativity and lead you to new ideas. Guiding the chatbot, you can modify the tone (e.g., casual, empathetic, persuasive, authoritative) and target the messaging to a unique audience (e.g., social media users, executives, influencers, thought leaders). With so many options, the sky is the limit!
- **Interests and experience.** Remember, you bring to the table your knowledge, life experience, and areas of expertise and curiosity as the starting point for any query. Without these you would have no perspective or point of view. Thankfully, your entire life has prepared you for this moment, so make sure to get off your digital devices, go outside, and live a little (or a lot)!
- **Empathy and passion.** AI supplies the information; you supply the heart. Your human capacity for empathy, caring, and compassion will make your communications uniquely human. Your passion for your topic will ring true as it resonates with your audience.

- **Judgment and decision-making.** Ultimately, you get to decide what to do with the information you learn from an AI chatbot. You can apply reason and meaning to the generated content. How do you feel about it? How will you use it to craft the story you want to tell? The results are automated, but the final product is entirely in your hands.

With AI taking over the more task-oriented things from our to-do lists, we will have more time to do more creative, higher-level work. In a lot of ways, it will make our work lives easier—or at least more meaningful and enriching—to get rid of tiresome lower-value tasks. Now you can put all your brainpower behind what matters most. I think many of us will be astonished to discover the gifts that come from working at a higher level.

Once again: this level of deep work can't happen without finding ways to bring a higher level of concentration and quiet into our daily lives. No longer can we struggle to focus in a noisy environment. Real change *must* happen. Won't it be ironic if the arrival of AI—the ultimate noisemaker— is what finally convinces us to ditch our self-destructive "TMI, TMC" ways and embrace a healthier, happier, more rewarding way of working and living?

The bullet train has left the station. You can't outrun it, so I hope you will hop on and sit in the quiet car for the ride.

## BRIEFLY STATED

AI is already here and influencing the world. The faster the world flies, the slower we need to go. We need more quiet to do uniquely human things computers can't do.

# QUIET CONSIDERATIONS

**DO I**: feel excited about, challenged by, or afraid of the introduction of AI in the workplace?

**WOULD I**: be comfortable and confident finding ways to utilize generative AI in my thinking and planning steps before communicating?

**CAN I**: challenge myself to apply the BRIEF steps to develop a plan for quiet query and to ask better questions while using AI technology?

# PART TWO

# QUIET ISN'T WHAT YOU THINK

Don't be complicated or a cynic when it comes to embracing moments of quiet in a hectic workday. It may seem like a luxury or an impossibility. Setting aside time for quiet is neither too technical nor practically impossible. Nor is the aim to achieve pure silence or to just attempt it at home or to go off the grid indefinitely and live a monk's life. The approach is simple: quiet starts by removing the noise.

# Chapter 6

# My Turning Point: How I Realized Quiet Was the Missing Piece

didn't wake up one day with a eureka moment about the importance of quiet. It was a gradual progression. I had already written my first book, *BRIEF: Make a Bigger Impact by Saying Less*, and was deep into writing my second book, *NOISE: Living and Leading When Nobody Can Focus*. Things were moving along nicely up to that point.

And then, when I got to chapter fourteen—which was titled "Quiet Time: Restoring and Recharging Your Mind"—I hit a wall. Here I was writing about the importance of managing all the noise that consumes our lives when I realized I was being a big hypocrite. How could I tell people to find daily quiet when I didn't even do it myself?

I stopped writing the chapter then and there. I decided I wouldn't keep going until I figured out exactly how to stop the chaos that noise creates for all of us. That's how I began my official journey to discover and embrace quiet.

It turned out I had my work cut out for me. I knew that quiet—intentional time dedicated to silence—was what was missing from the workday. But I needed to practice what I preached in order to prove its effectiveness.

I started by doing a lot of research. I studied meditation and mindfulness and soon fell down a rabbit hole exploring various techniques and exercises to help quiet my mind.

Well, things got really technical really fast. Everything I tried felt complicated and arduous. It felt performative, and I was always extremely conscious of how I was doing at any given moment. Not only that, but the techniques also weren't really working for me. My inner world felt noisier, not quieter. Regardless of whether I was doing my breathing exercises or desperately trying to clear my mind of all thoughts, I couldn't wait to finish. Things were going so badly that I was starting to feel I couldn't use quiet as a tool for noise management.

I kept banging my head against the wall until I stumbled upon the first breakthrough that would set me on a path to discovering the truth about quiet. It came in the form of a quote from English writer G. K. Chesterton:

**Insight #1: Anything worth doing in life is worth doing badly.** Wow. This spoke to me, and suddenly I understood: it's okay to be bad at being quiet.

Chesterton was telling us that performance doesn't matter. Quiet doesn't have to be mastered or perfected. We can do it "badly," and that's okay. This insight helped me immediately remove the self-judgment I had been feeling. I didn't need to worry about getting a B instead of an A … or even an F! It was okay to be terrible at it. What was important was showing up and doing it.

That brought me to my second powerful insight.

**Insight #2: It's not a technique. It's an appointment.** There's no right or wrong way of doing quiet. We don't need to study or learn any specific technique to experience quiet—which, remember, is simply the absence of noise. What's important is making time to lower the noise and sticking with it no matter what.

## My Turning Point: How I Realized Quiet Was the Missing Piece

I started making appointments with myself for quiet time. Initially, I started with five to ten minutes and treated them the way I would any other appointment, like a teeth cleaning or a meeting with my boss. They were opportunities to tune out the noise and do the thinking, planning, and preparing that I needed to be successful in my workday. Instead of worrying about *how* I would use the appointment, I focused simply on showing up for it. Sticking to my appointments for quiet was more important than worrying about how I spent the time.

When I discovered this insight, everything started to make sense. I suddenly understood why people sometimes struggled to implement my ideas in my first book, *BRIEF*. They weren't utilizing quiet to prepare for their communication and collaboration. Instead, they were thinking, speaking, and doing *on the fly*. Silence really was the missing ingredient for so many professionals.

**Insight #3: One thing at a time.** I soon came to realize I was doing too many things at once. So I started focusing on only one thing at a time during my quiet appointment. I would think. Or read. Or choose. Or dream. Or plan. Or listen. Or complain.

You get the picture. Just one thing.

We should do it this way because our minds are fast; just because we can think of many things at once doesn't mean we should operate in that state—especially not during quiet. Our busy, noisy minds are like a treadmill running at a high speed. When we get off that treadmill, our bodies want to keep running. So to get off safely, we have to slow down and then come to a stop. Doing only one thing at a time is the slowdown our minds are craving.

These insights allowed me to give myself permission to embrace my quiet experiment without worry. Instead of trying to do it the "right" way, I abandoned the rules and did whatever it was that I needed to do in each appointment. I let myself do it "badly" and relaxed into it. It wasn't half bad.

Here are some of the ways I started spending my quiet time at work:

**Planning.** On Mondays I would use my quiet time for planning my week. It became a good way for me to think about upcoming priorities, goals, and deadlines and make a game plan.

**Reading.** I would spend time in the afternoon reading or listening to an audiobook. Anyone who wants to work on their craft and grow needs to keep learning and keep reading, but most of us rarely or never read at work. Even a ten-minute pocket of quiet spent reading teaches us new things we can use to further our career.

**Doing nothing.** When work got especially hectic or chaotic, I would take a time-out to do nothing. Literally. I would stare at a wall. I intentionally cleared my mind of all mental tasks. This was my way of hitting "mute" on the noise.

**Complaining.** Sometimes the workday can take a negative or stressful turn. When things became particularly challenging, I would let myself moan and complain by talking to myself about challenges, issues, and obstacles I was experiencing. It was extremely impactful because I could get the negativity out of my system and move on. Goodbye, prolonged stewing and ruminating!

**Making a list.** A list is a great way to contain your thoughts. For instance, whenever I felt overwhelmed because there was a lot going on, I would make a list of what I felt grateful for in that moment—shoes, running water, automatic ice makers, etc. Building a list like this helped me both manage the noise and also remember that even when my life was tough, it was still awesome. Keep in mind that you can make other kinds of lists as well (to-do lists, grocery lists, etc.)

**Looking back.** Quiet time became a great opportunity for me to take a scan of the previous workday, or the previous meeting, or the conversation I just had with a colleague. Without reflection, we don't learn. I found so much value in looking back over time I might have otherwise forgotten.

I carried on like this for a while, discovering all the different ways I could use this time. Then something great happened. I started finding tremendous value in my short quiet appointments. They stopped being an obligation and became something I looked forward to. At the end of my appointments, I found myself wanting to stay in the quiet longer. And I noticed that I was performing better than ever.

Before long I was taking a half hour at the beginning of the business day and a half hour at the end to have quiet. Now, this won't be the right amount of time for everyone, but it is what works for me. It's how I get my head right for the day ahead and how I transition out of the workday at the end. And it's been life-changing, both personally and professionally.

Several months into my practice, I started realizing this was something from which everyone could benefit, and I couldn't wait to share it with others—not only for their benefit, but also for the benefit of organizations everywhere. At first it was just me doing quiet as my own personal journey. But then I discovered that if we want to change how an organization behaves, we've got to get a lot of people to do it at the same time. One person alone can't change the culture. But many people can together.

Now you know how I came to realize quiet was what was missing from work. And hopefully you're beginning to recognize the value it could have in your own career and life. In the remainder of part two of *Quiet Works*, we'll get really clear on what quiet is and what it isn't.

## BRIEFLY STATED

Anything worth doing in life is worth doing badly, so challenge yourself to make an appointment to "do" some quiet—but don't pressure yourself to do it "right." Focus on only one thing at a time during your newly found quiet time and allow your mind time for a slowdown.

## QUIET CONSIDERATIONS

**DO I**: have a "monkey brain" that just won't turn off?

**WOULD I**: accept that this practice of quiet time can be challenging and give myself a chance to fail at it before I get better at it?

**CAN I**: begin to carve out time for quiet reflection and planning and make it part of my daily routine?

## Chapter 7

# Words of Wisdom and Why We Run from Quiet

When I first began experimenting with quiet, I wanted to find out what others had to say about it. Surely I wasn't the first person to make the connection that solitude and silence are catalysts for growth, creativity, increased performance, and renewal. So I started to dig. As I have stated previously, my research took me to some surprising places. Some a little weird and wacky, and some far too esoteric for my tastes. Others made no sense but sounded like they did (maybe to themselves!). But I did find several pearls of wisdom that resonated with me.

Turns out, silence has long been revered by many notable figures throughout history. These insights aren't anything new. Wise people have known about and shared the value of quiet, silence, solitude—whatever you want to call it—way before the digital age filled with distractions and devices. The wisdom has always existed, but it has been largely forgotten because there's not enough room for it in our noisy world. Until and unless we make room for it, nothing will change, so we must learn from the past.

The insights of the best and brightest minds that precede us are more relevant now than ever before. We can't afford for them to be lost forever.

In fact, we should embrace time alone with a new sense of urgency if we want to keep thinking, dreaming, creating, and innovating.

But don't take my word for it. Let's read on and learn from some of history's most prominent thinkers.

### Blaise Pascal: French philosopher, mathematician, and author of *Pensées*

"All of humanity's problems stem from man's inability to sit quietly in a room alone." This quote is about going to the source of the problem. Stop moving. Stop talking. It's the constant movement and constant communication that cause so many of our problems. Quiet, the antidote, lowers the noise.

### Thomas Merton: American Trappist monk and author

"The solitary life, being silent, clears away the smoke-screen of words that man has laid down between his mind and things."[1] Words can create clutter; they can often create a barrier between what we are thinking and living. Quiet clears away the smoke screen of words. Solitude helps you get at what matters most.

### Francis Bacon: English philosopher

"Silence is the sleep that nourishes wisdom." Silence is an opportunity to foster a growth mindset. It is about creating time to reflect, rejuvenate, and find clarity. This is a good reminder to take moments of silence for reflection in our noisy world.

### William Penn: English founder of Pennsylvania

"True silence is the rest of the mind, and is to the spirit what sleep is to the body, nourishment and refreshment." In the same way our bodies need sleep for restoration, our minds need quiet for renewal. After being worked all day, they need a break.

**Confucius: Chinese philosopher**
"Silence is a true friend who never betrays." Spending a little (or a lot of) time in quiet is always beneficial to us. It never hurts (even if we are a little afraid of it). Trust in that friendship.

**Nikola Tesla: Serbian American inventor**
"Originality thrives in seclusion free of outside influences beating upon us to cripple the creative mind. Be alone, that is the secret of invention; be alone, that is when ideas are born." During our time alone, we can reflect and think creatively, rather than diluting our attention with an endless number of distractions. Find the peace of being alone—make time for wondering and creative ideas.

**Albert Einstein: German/Swiss theoretical physicist**
"The monotony and solitude of a quiet life stimulates the creative mind." Einstein—probably a lot like Stephen Hawking—spent much of his time thinking about things. Remember, he also famously said, "It's not that I'm so smart, it's just that I stay with problems longer." Now, I would bet that Einstein *was* significantly more intelligent than a lot of people, but the time he spent quietly thinking about solutions no doubt contributed to his reputation greatly.

**Napoleon Hill: American author**
"Wise men, when in doubt whether to speak or to keep quiet, give themselves the benefit of the doubt, and remain silent." Quiet gives us the opportunity for self-control; sometimes it's truly best to say nothing at all.

**Stephen Hawking: English theoretical physicist**
"Quiet people have the loudest minds." Those with the most brilliant minds (whether recognized publicly for it or not) spend a lot of time thinking. Their voices may be quiet, but their minds are endlessly active.

## Quiet Works

### Steve Jobs: American businessman
"Don't let the noise of others' opinions drown out your own inner voice." Staying true to yourself is tough work, especially if you spend too much time dwelling on other people's opinions. Jobs reminds us that we need to follow our inner voice. Quiet allows us to return to our original thoughts and gives us time to reflect and create without judgment.

### Warren Buffett: American businessman
"I just sit in my office and read all day." This practice seems completely counterintuitive in today's connected business world. Yet quiet time for reading and thinking can help one to make better, less impulsive decisions, paving the way for success.

### Susan Cain: American writer and lecturer
"The secret to life is to put yourself in the right lighting. For some, it's a Broadway spotlight; for others, a lamplit desk. Use your natural powers—of persistence, concentration, and insight—to do work you love and work that matters. Solve problems. Make art. Think deeply." Individuals should embrace their ingrained strengths, including the need for quiet and focus to go deeper.

### Mother Teresa: Albanian Indian Catholic nun and saint
"We need to find God, and he cannot be found in noise and restlessness. God is the friend of silence. See how nature—trees, flowers, grass—grows in silence ... We need silence to be able to touch souls." Silence and solitude are prerequisites for being able to grow.

### Thomas Carlyle: English essayist, historian, and philosopher
"Speech is silver. Silence is golden." Saying nothing at times is commendable. Discretion is impactful.

**Epictetus: Greek philosopher**
"Keep silence for the most part, and speak only when you must, and then briefly." Take time to reflect and consider, and then present a clear, concise message.

**Isaiah: Major prophet of the Old Testament**
"For thus said the Lord GOD, the Holy One of Israel, 'In returning and rest you shall be saved; in quietness and in trust shall be your strength'" (Isaiah 30:15, English Standard Version). There's power in coming back to moments of quiet to restore and regain our strength.

To learn more, check out the *Just Saying* podcast, episode "Seven Words of Wisdom on Silence to Savor": podcast .thebrieflab.com/ep-293-seven-words-of-wisdom-on-silence -to-savor.

These are timeless thoughts, but they are so very suitable for us today. To move as fast as we need to in our modern age, we have to (ironically) slow down and look backward. Some of the people quoted above lived in what we would consider a fairly quiet world, with no internet, electricity, or smartphones. If they celebrated the need for quiet, we should all heed their advice. And yet most people will go to great lengths to avoid quiet whenever the opportunity presents itself.

## If We Crave Quiet, Why Do We Avoid It at All Costs?

Most people will tell you that they'd do almost anything for some peace and quiet. They *say* they would love to escape the noise—that they're craving a long, blissful stretch of silence. But when you get down to it, what people say and what they do are two different things.

First, most people don't really want quiet. It makes them feel nervous or maybe even afraid. Think about it: we're so conditioned to be around people, to constantly seek input or buy-in and navigate chaos, that we slowly back away from our own company.

Heck no, we *don't* welcome quiet! It's more accurate to say we run from it!

Second, quiet isn't really the escape that most people envision or romanticize—especially when it comes to quiet in the workplace. We equate quiet with relaxing on a deserted beach or getting away for a long walk in the woods. The kind of quiet I'm describing isn't a "Calgon, take me away!" moment. It's not always, or even often, easy. It depends on your ability to focus, think, and deal with tough problems. Deep down, some part of us already knows this, which is why even when we have the rare chance for some quiet, we find ways to avoid it.

The bottom line is, quiet isn't easy. It can take you to some places you'd rather not be. But I promise you it's worth exploring, and when utilized correctly, it can change your life and your career.

Here's a list of the top reasons why we avoid quiet, in no particular order. Some of them will resonate with you more than others. That's to be expected because we've all got unique circumstances and life experiences. But don't be surprised if you find yourself nodding in agreement with many of these insights.

**Reason #1: Quiet can be super uncomfortable.** Quiet can feel awkward, *especially* when you are first getting used to it. It's jarring to suddenly jump off the hamster wheel and simply stop. You are used to being surrounded by people and technology, and suddenly there's no sound and no company. You'll likely feel tempted to jump back into the fray, and you'll need to resist in order to stick with it! (As a side note, this is one of those times when our introverted colleagues might fare better than extroverts. Those who savor their alone time may feel right at home in quiet.) For the rest of us, keep pushing through the discomfort. I promise it will be worth it.

**Reason #2: The focused work associated with quiet is often hard.** Embracing quiet can be tricky. That's because things like thinking and focusing are difficult. When it's time for quiet, our brains start running ninety miles an hour and our Elusive 600 (see below), which I touched on in depth in *NOISE*, is on fire. Further, we are often too overwhelmed from the sheer volume of information coming toward us to buckle down and focus. In a Steelcase article titled "The Privacy Crisis: Taking a Toll on Employee Engagement," performance-management consultant and author David Rock shares: "Science has shown that the human prefrontal cortex, where most knowledge work processes take place, is small, energy-hungry and very easily distracted." And if you thought multitasking could save you, think again: "Many researchers' work has proven that any belief that people can multitask is essentially wishful thinking," the article continues. "Humans can give controlled, full attention to just one thing at a time. When we try to pay attention actively to any two memory-dependent tasks at once, we're easily distracted and end up doing neither one well."[2] Finally, our perception of time changes depending on whether we are doing busy work or quiet work. Research reveals that the same amount of time feels longer when we are doing focused work than it does when we are doing busy work.[3]

The Elusive 600 is a core concept I learned from my good friend and communications expert Sharon Ellis. Our brains process about 750 words a minute, while the average person only speaks or reads about 150 words a minute. Our brains essentially over-process by six hundred words per minute. In this context it's easy to see why quiet feels so hard. When we are reading, thinking, or doing another quiet activity, our internal monologue often has

> other plans. It takes practice and discipline to silence the Elusive
> 600 and go about our quiet work. (But even on days that you can't
> fully tone down the internal noise, remember that quiet is always
> worth doing—even when we do it "badly"!)

**Reason #3: It seems unproductive.** So many of us equate our self-worth with busyness. Our default mode is one of action and checking things off our list. Quiet, on the other hand, feels passive and unproductive. You may feel like you're doing nothing or that it's a waste of time. It might even feel like a luxury, one we can't quite justify. But one of the big lessons this book will teach you is that even when you're doing "nothing," you're still doing "something." And that "something" will have a tremendous impact on your life.

**Reason #4: "People don't give me permission."** When your environment, or the people you work alongside, do not let you step away for quiet, it can truly feel unattainable. Someone is always knocking on our door, texting, calling, or emailing us, and we don't have autonomy to change that. Further, open work offices may not even have doors! A 2023 *Forbes Australia* article shares that "over 95% of the workforce say they are interrupted at least 3 or 4 times per day and it takes 23 minutes and 15 seconds to fully recover focus after a distraction. And let's not talk about the 30 odd hours a month we are spending in unproductive meetings."[4] Finally, most workplaces have no established boundaries or social norms around giving people quiet, uninterrupted time for thinking and deep work.

**Reason #5: Tech is all around (and we're addicted to it).** It's nearly impossible to escape technology. Screens are everywhere no matter where we go. And even if we could somehow escape our tech-driven environment, we don't really *want* to. It's too tempting to pick up our phones or get on the computer and binge on useless information. In *NOISE*, I compared it to consuming a diet of Diet Coke and popcorn all day long—totally delicious, but insubstantial. It leaves us empty and hangry for something more filling.

**Reason #6: Quiet is not habit or routine... yet.** Quiet is hard for us because we're just not used to it. It's something we occasionally might experience (and when we do, we probably enjoy it), but it's not something we view as important or schedule on a daily basis. On the other hand, our calendars are chock-full of collaborative appointments and opportunities to consume information. And because that's our norm, we passively perpetuate it.

**Reason #7: "I'm afraid of what I'll find."** Many of us are afraid of being alone and going deeper into our souls and psyches. Quiet is a chance to sit with our thoughts and reflect, but in doing so we might find things that are difficult or traumatizing, or things that we simply don't want to face right now. Loved ones die, relationships end, financial crises loom, and silence gives us a sometimes unwelcome opportunity to dredge up these events or memories. And, of course, there's the biggie to consider: our own mortality. So instead we stay busy because a distracted mind allows us to avoid the really deep, intense stuff that might be scary or painful or hard.

**Reason #8: "I don't know what to do or how to do it."** We know how to tie our shoes and wash our hands, but the techniques around quiet are elusive and foreign. Do we stare at the wall? Count sheep? It feels mysterious because we haven't had much experience with quiet and because no one is talking about its importance—until now! Remember, anything worth doing in life is worth doing badly. Give it a try—*your* way!

**Reason #9: There's nowhere to go that's distraction free.** Even when we want to have quiet, where do we go to get it? When so many offices have open floor plans, a collaborative culture, or both, it can be nearly impossible to find a place we can be alone. In many workplaces, even working from home, there's no escape from the noise. I've heard so many people tell me, "The only place I can find any quiet is in the bathroom." It's sad but true. We desperately need better options. Employees deserve to do their thinking in a flush-free zone!

**Reason #10: Quiet is "boring."** Most of us like to spend our time doing things that are fun, fulfilling, and full of immediate gratification. At first glance, quiet doesn't seem to check these boxes. It can feel tedious, boring, and out of sync with what we are used to (especially when it's new to us). Last of all, there's little immediate payoff. Most people would prefer to be playing a game on their phone, or checking an email, or listening to a podcast. Given all this, it's no surprise that quiet doesn't appear to measure up.

So yes, there are plenty of reasons you likely shy away—okay, run away—from quiet. Even on the rare occasion you that you have dipped your toe into the waters of quiet, you probably didn't stay there long. And now you know why.

Take some time to understand which of the above reasons resonate most with you. You owe it to yourself to think about the impact of not addressing these feelings or beliefs. Yes, quiet *can* be uncomfortable, boring, or confusing, and it goes against the grain of workplace culture. But those aren't good enough reasons to stay away. There are too many good things that come from it.

Changing your habits won't be a cakewalk. You will need to grapple with tough questions in order to embrace new routines and reap the benefits of quiet. This means drilling down on your beliefs, habits, and fears by asking things like:

- What do I do to face things that are difficult?
- What does it really mean to be productive?
- How can I gain greater autonomy?
- Where can I find a quiet space?
- Do I only do things that are fun and fulfilling?
- What do I do when I get bored?

The answers to these questions will be illuminating. Wait and see. You'll learn a lot about yourself, about where you are now, and about where you could go.

Our next chapter will build on what you've learned here and help separate fact from fiction. I'm going to challenge some popular yet limiting beliefs and get clear on what quiet is and what it is not.

It's time to stop running and learn why quiet works.

## BRIEFLY STATED

While great thinkers throughout history have valued quiet, there are many reasons why people run from it today. Quiet doesn't come easily, but by facing the challenge of trusting ourselves to find moments of solitude, we can get past the barriers and open our minds to new habits.

## QUIET CONSIDERATIONS

**DO I:** avoid quiet because I am afraid of it, because I don't have time for it, or because I don't know how to get started?

**WOULD I:** benefit from a workplace that not only encourages quiet but also includes designated spaces to work, think, and plan in quiet?

**CAN I:** stop trying to fill my waking hours with random tasks or meaningless engagements and plan times for thinking and deep work?

Chapter 8

# Knowing What Quiet Is and Isn't (It's *Not* a Technique; It's an Appointment)

One of the biggest barriers you might encounter along this quiet journey is misunderstanding what *quiet* really means. In chapter one you learned that quiet is the daily practice of setting aside time for solitary focused work *and* a method of pausing to think instead of speaking on the fly. But beyond that, many people are unclear on how to "do" quiet time, and they're also fuzzy on the deeper implications of quiet. For some, quiet is far too squishy an idea to take seriously. Others may feel like it's a luxury they can't afford. ("Who has time to sit and think? I've got work to do!")

Those views are totally understandable but still superficial. We may think quiet is having the time to frolic through a meadow counting daisy petals or staring at a wall in an empty room. But the truth is, most people's preconceived notions around quiet are misplaced. (And costly ones at that, because they might prevent you from taking action that leads to growth.)

Quiet isn't fluffy and fanciful. Nor is it something you must master. You don't need to dedicate ten thousand hours of your precious time to practicing a specific technique. Heck, you don't have to do it perfectly, or even well!

Instead, quiet is an appointment you make time for each day no matter what. As little as five or ten minutes can create changes that you and others will notice in your performance, focus, communication, and much more.

It's what professionals desperately need.

Now let's drill down to the real meaning of quiet. It's something far simpler and far more powerful than you might think. Here are some considerations:

**Quiet isn't Zen or a "Calgon moment."** It's not something you do at home, dazed and spent after the Sturm und Drang of the day. In the context of this book, quiet is something that happens at work, that advances work, and that makes work better. It's not overtly about well-being (though, done regularly, it will improve well-being).

**Quiet isn't talking.** Okay ... this one is pretty obvious. But it deserves to be said because most of us have a strong urge to fill silences with chatter. Yet when you and others stop talking, there's momentary relief. Embrace it. It gives us, and those around us, a break. Consider coworkers, collaborators, and clients as occasional beneficiaries of your self-control. It may be a way to help you help them.

**Quiet is listening.** Embracing silence can enhance our ability to be present and listen to understand others better. Research shows that people spend between 50 percent and 80 percent of their workday engaged in some form of communication,[1] and about 55 percent of their time is devoted to listening.[2] But do they actively listen? When we actively engage in attentive silence, we give others the space to express themselves fully without interruption or judgment. This not only strengthens our relationships but also deepens our understanding of different perspectives and fosters empathy.

**Quiet is difficult.** Don't let the difficulty surprise you. The impulse toward noise is easy and strong. The adage "no pain, no gain" is true when it comes to forgoing the urge to communicate, and slowing down to carefully consider, reflect, and concentrate. In our noisy world, this is awkward, and we need to face that challenge head-on.

**Quiet isn't pure silence.** Quiet is defined as the absence of noise, but don't confuse this with absolute silence. Imagine you're in a quiet restaurant: there's a low murmur of voices, soft music, and the clink of silverware. None of this is distracting. It's calming and enjoyable. Now imagine that the restaurant is absolutely silent. How strange that would be! Our goal is to remove distractions, and realistically we can't get rid of them all.

**Quiet is both auditory and visual.** Distractions come in the form of audible noise, but they also appear in visual cues. If you're in an environment that is loud, you can't help but hear it all. The same is true if you're surrounded by countless things you can see, like screens, people, pictures, and movement. Closing your eyes can be as powerful as closing your ears.

**Quiet is a choice.** When working, we often thoughtlessly move toward a steady state of collaboration: checking email, sending messages, talking with coworkers, running from meeting to meeting, and just staying busy—and connected—at all times. To get off the hamster wheel, you need to decide to jump off. If not, the mindless momentum will carry you through the entire workday.

**Quiet isn't just occasional.** For most professionals, quiet time comes unexpectedly—maybe when they are waiting for someone who's late for a meeting, or in the office when people are away at a conference. Even though there may be many unforeseen moments like those, we need to make setting aside time for deep work a priority, not just a rarity.

**Quiet isn't for when you're not busy.** The more demanding your schedule, the more critical quiet is. There's always a temptation: "I'll get to it when I have more time; I'm too busy to slow down right now." The busier you are, the more you need to slow down. The psychoanalyst Erich Fromm observed that "modern man thinks he loses something—time—when he does not do things quickly; yet he does not know what to do with the time he gains—except kill it." You're trying to catch a bullet train by running alongside of it. That's absurd! Get inside the train and you'll be going just as fast, but it will seem slow.

**Quiet isn't a technique.** What works for someone else may never work for you. Learn what suits you. The biggest temptation is to treat quiet like a series of weird practices that are forced and foreign to you. If you fall prey to that, you will abandon quiet altogether. Remember: *you can't do quiet the wrong way.* Lowering the noise, even a little—and imperfectly—is always good.

**Quiet is an appointment.** Schedule time every day where you plan for quiet, not hope for it. Professionals live by schedules, and the busier they get, the more important managing the calendar becomes. It can fill in top to bottom with constant collaboration and no room for thinking, leaving you to just do everything on the fly between meetings. If quiet is essential (it is), then treat it like any other appointment—and don't cancel it when something (or someone) else comes calling. Hold firm.

**Quiet is always useful.** You'll never regret spending time in silence. Consider all the things you do at work that end up being a waste of time: sitting in meetings, responding to messages, listening to your boss drone on, multitasking. So much of it can be a tragic time drain. Quiet is never that way because your mind needs a break from all the noise. When you run all day, pausing is always productive.

**Quiet isn't for immediate gratification.** No, you probably won't see a quick payoff. Setting aside five minutes between meetings for quiet or taking a minute to collect your thoughts before starting a task may feel unproductive in the moment. "I'm in such a hurry," you say instinctively. "I can't afford to stop right now." But the opposite is true: each quiet moment is an investment that will generate an enormous return over time.

**Quiet is restorative.** When people do a tough workout, there's generally a recovery day. If not, they can get injured more easily and sidelined, forced to recover. Our brains are working nonstop, jumping from one stimulus to another and back, taking a toll on our ability to concentrate. We need to give it a rest, slow down the machine, and let it cool off and rebuild.

**Quiet is what lowers noise.** It's both a noun *and* a verb. You actively quiet—reduce—noise by choice. You do something to lower the distractions and disruptions by consciously deciding to turn the knob down. Don't feel helpless; do something now. Stop being passive, helplessly waiting for quiet (the noun) to arrive. Be active and confidently quiet (the verb) your work environment.

**Quiet isn't for a grade.** Don't worry about doing it well. What matters is not missing it. When we think about performing at a high level, we get frustrated when we're not perfect. If we feel like we're falling short, we may abandon our efforts. Noise is a brutal adversary that doesn't want you to fight back. If we stop thinking about getting an A+, we will always defend ourselves and come out winners.

## Quiet Works

**Quiet is a conversation with yourself.** We talk to ourselves constantly. Sometimes these internal conversations can be extremely insightful, productive, and revealing. Other times, it may be pretty defeating to listen to a negative monologue. Instead of allowing your thoughts to run wild and unchecked, it is important to be more deliberate with these conversations. Being more purposeful about the things you say to yourself helps you maintain a positive mindset and make better decisions. During your quiet time, listen to how you talk to yourself and the truths (and lies) you say inaudibly. Those conversations can be very telling.

**Quiet isn't transactional.** Thinking isn't just about results and being better at getting more things done. Sometimes the best thing to do is nothing. It may seem useless, but quiet isn't always about a quick hit. It's more relational than transactional. It's about thinking before saying something. It's about looking back and forward. It's about treating yourself as a person, not a machine.

**Quiet is transformative.** Over time, these precious times spent in quiet will change you profoundly. The habit of slowing down, investing precious time, and being more intentional will change you not only as a professional but also as a person. Specifically, it simply got me to pay attention to more important matters and stop chasing useless things beyond my reach. It allowed me to hone my craft and stop wasting time on what depleted me professionally. Please remember that others depend on you to be the best version of yourself. Living with quiet will make that happen in a profound and powerful way.

**Quiet isn't weird.** Any time that you see people treating quiet in strange ways, feel sorry for them. There's a tendency to take something that is simple, wholesome, and good and try to unnecessarily complicate it. By doing so, we just end up creating a world of weirdness that's uninviting. Why would we want to embrace quiet if that meant performing odd practices that make us look eccentric? It is a professional practice that doesn't look odd or off-putting. Be quiet and be normal.

**Quiet is what makes us more human.** Carefully consider a life without quiet: it's not much of a life. As the world blends deeply and rapidly with technology in unplanned, unexpected, and scary ways, we need to do what makes us uniquely human: give ourselves time to reflect, imagine, feel, decide, mourn, hope, believe, strive, create, and remember. That's worthwhile.

I hope you're feeling encouraged and hopeful after reading this list. You don't have to become a yogi or a monk to start a quiet practice. You don't need unlimited time and energy. You don't need a cabin in the wilderness. You *do* need to make quiet a priority. And you do need to give yourself permission to take that oh-so-precious pause. (See chapter ten for all the details!)

But don't worry—once you begin seeing the tangible results quiet delivers, you'll never want to stop.

## BRIEFLY STATED

Clarifying what quiet is and is not can help us discover how to make it a priority. Remember: It is a technique, not an appointment. And it's always worthwhile.

> ## QUIET CONSIDERATIONS
>
> **DO I:** avoid moments of quiet because I don't know how to "do" quiet?
>
> **WOULD I:** gain confidence in my ability to practice quiet by eliminating specific visual and auditory distractions in my workplace?
>
> **CAN I:** give others the gift of present listening and gain the reputation as a generous, attentive, considerate colleague?

# PART THREE

# QUIET PRACTICES
# AT WORK

It's easy for professionals to say they want some quiet, but in a noisy world people generally avoid it. Succumbing to distractions, devices, and diversions is easier. Yet embracing quiet, however challenging it might be, and sitting still stops the cycle. Instead of running, we realize that time spent in quiet has a power. There are practical ways to set aside time every day for it and begin to realize how silence can become the secret ingredient in our workday.

# Chapter 9

# Principles and Practices: Defining What You Believe Will Shape How You Behave

When you think of a productive workplace, what comes to mind? If you're like most people, you might picture a bustling bullpen where employees are talking, typing, and moving about with purpose. For sure everyone *looks* busy and on task. Now imagine a person sitting at their desk reading. Or quietly thinking for an extended period of time. These activities wouldn't look like work at all. They would look like leisure, daydreaming, or even laziness.

By now you don't need a spoiler alert to tell you these activities aren't pointless or useless at all. In fact, they are a crucial part of the workday. And yet we do not give ourselves or others permission to do them. Instead, we default to talk-to-talk and create nonstop noise.

Why?

*Because we have bought into lies that have sabotaged our ability to do meaningful work.*

Most people's beliefs around work are deeply flawed. We may

intuitively know that doing good work requires periods of solitude, rest, and quiet, but we also must keep up the appearance of busyness to uphold the culture of constant activity and collaboration that most organizations embrace. To succeed (or even just survive), we join the dysfunction. Before we know it, we have absorbed and adopted a wildly flawed set beliefs and behaviors.

Here's a short list of our careless conclusions:

- If you're sitting still and not doing something, you're not working.
- Collaboration is always useful, and you can only get work done by having other people around.
- Everyone in the work environment should be an extrovert.
- Staying connected to technology is essential at every moment of the day.
- You should drop everything when your colleagues come calling and give them your full attention.
- People are more comfortable being busy than being thoughtful.
- You should always be accessible, no matter where you are.

Not only are these beliefs flawed, but they also don't serve us at all! In fact, they make us less productive and more stressed.

Think about it. Does it really benefit you or your organization for you to be available to others at the drop of a hat? Or, as a leader, do you have that expectation for others? I worked with a client where a simple misunderstanding led employees in the company to feel the pressure of this expectation of availability. They believed the CEO wanted them to be available 24/7 since he would set deadlines for EOD (end of day). To him, EOD was midnight—he felt he was giving the employees more freedom and flexibility to get their work done with extended time. Unfortunately, the employees felt pressure to work or be available until his EOD. Talk about more stress! Can you really be more productive when you never have a break from meetings and tasks? Does the *appearance* of busyness really make you more valuable to your company?

Of course not. Beliefs and behaviors like these perpetuate the toxic culture of work. They lead to burnout and exhaustion. And they prevent creativity and innovation that all companies need to be successful in a competitive business environment. That's why we need to overhaul the "rule book" and adopt a new way of being and working.

> *It's time to change the conversation about the role of quiet in the workplace. That starts with challenging our counterproductive beliefs.*

Why? Because changing what we believe will change how we behave. It's time to reject the lies we've swallowed and move away from the toxic culture that makes us unproductive and miserable. One person alone can't do it; everyone must take part. When we all work together, the shift will be powerful and effective.

## Seven Principles and Practices That Make Fulfilling, Meaningful Work Possible

Here is a simple set of core beliefs and principles that will guide you toward moments of consistent quiet and help set the tone for a workplace that works for everyone:

1. **Attention is a scarce resource that needs to be protected.** Focus on one thing at a time and avoid the temptation to multitask. Protect your attention from distraction.

2. **Quiet is a powerful ingredient in our personal and professional lives.** Just a few minutes can set the tone for the day. Let people know when you need it. Post "do not disturb" signs that let others know not to interrupt or distract you.

3. **Quiet deserves a dedicated space.** Being surrounded by screens and interruptions won't cut it. Designate a specific area at the office, in your home, or on the road as your own quiet workplace.

4. **Quiet deserves a scheduled time.** Schedule specific moments for quiet time and treat them as nonnegotiable appointments. Remember, it's less about your technique and more about consistently making quiet happen.

5. **Technology isn't always necessary.** Take tech time-outs during the day, especially at the start and end.

6. **Collaboration isn't always beneficial.** Have portions of the day reserved for deep work. Don't interrupt people during these times. In meetings, provide silent starts so everyone is in the right mindset before they begin talking.

7. **Not everything is an an emergency.** Say, "No, not now" more often by having concrete criteria of what is actually urgent and important.

We've come to a point where something needs to change. It's overdue. Technology made it possible to communicate 24/7 and for work to begin encroaching on our private lives. Open floor plans literally tore down the walls between us, and we can be distracted and disturbed by anyone, anytime. Having fewer boundaries has backfired. Instead of making us more efficient and productive, the flood of noise has destroyed our ability to do our best work.

But you've got the power to make things right. First for you. Then for your organization.

Change begins at the individual level. Over the next several chapters, we'll dig deeper into tactics you can use to make quiet work for you.

These principles and practices are the first steps. Use them as a blueprint to change your mindset and start building your autonomy.

## BRIEFLY STATED

We need to call out the lies we have about work and productivity and make both personal and institutional changes.

## QUIET CONSIDERATIONS

**DO I:** find myself falling into the trap of assuming those who are sitting quietly are less productive?

**WOULD I:** benefit from implementing one or two of the seven practices listed in this chapter to make fulfilling, meaningful work a part of my daily routine?

**CAN I:** flip my mindset and accept that I need to jump off the hamster wheel of appearing busy?

Chapter 10

# Permission to Pause: The Discipline to Do Nothing

've got some bad news: as much as we humans need daily quiet to achieve our professional best, no one is going to give us permission to take breaks and step away from the constant collaboration. The decision to take this crucial time to reflect, plan, prepare, or regroup is entirely up to you.

I can almost hear you now. "Joe, how hard can it possibly be to give myself a break?"

The truth is, it's harder than it seems. Think about the hectic nature of the workplace. Our list of priorities never ends. Clients need servicing; leaders are constantly in our ear demanding that we reach our goals; projects still need managing; we must put out fire after fire; my inbox keeps on filling. With all this pressure, taking a break to do nothing can feel impossible, unrealistic, and irresponsible.

But hear me out. It's precisely those moments when you're busy that you *must* stop for quiet.

Think back to one of those days when so many things happened that you couldn't even recall what you said and did once it was over. I remember plenty of times when my day was ceaseless movement, motion, comments, talking, conference calls, and meetings. It all felt like a blur.

One such time for me was when we celebrated all of our staff and families at a dual event for the company's tenth anniversary of The BRIEF Lab paired with an introduction of our Quiet Workplace—our new companion business. If there was ever a time in my career when I was running around like my hair was on fire, it was that day. I had an event to organize. I had to plan and lead a workshop for our facilitators who were coming into town. I had to write a toast for an evening dinner. It was during this time that I *had* to do quiet time—it was on my calendar. So I reserved a time in our Quiet Workplace, checked in, sat in one of the quiet pods, and got in the right mindset. It is easy to cancel appointments for quiet during our most hectic times, but busy people need to take moments of quiet, *especially* when they're busy.

Quiet can save us during such days. Giving yourself permission to pause makes all your experiences—even the hectic ones—far more valuable. It opens up time and space for insight, rest, inspiration, and more. It allows you to be deliberate in the chaos.

The phrase "permission to pause" was inspired by the great Patrick Lencioni. His book *The Advantage: Why Organizational Health Trumps Everything Else in Business* discusses core values leaders and employees must embrace. One of those core values is the "permission to play." When I read that, I felt a zap of inspiration, and "permission to pause" was born.

It means exactly what it sounds like. You can't wait for someone else to give you permission to take a time-out. You must make your own opportunities to stop, to do nothing. And don't be afraid to take a *significant* pause. This isn't like making a rolling stop like some drivers do. It's a complete stop. A pause in which there is no work, no activity, no busyness.

You can give yourself permission to pause during any moment you can think of. A short (or slightly longer) pause is a powerful way to become much more intentional in your thinking and be more present in that moment.

Pausing becomes a lot easier with practice. Here is a list of moments when you could give yourself permission to pause. With each of these examples, think specifically about when you would take a pause, and for how long.

## A Variety of Valuable Moments to Pause

**In the middle of a thought.** Yes, you can pause during a thought—any kind of thought. Sometimes we have random thoughts, and sometimes we have thoughts we shouldn't be thinking. Pausing allows you to consider those trains of thought and redirect them if necessary.

**When you're talking in a conversation.** When might it be valuable to take a pause? Maybe you need to give the other person a chance to speak. Maybe it's time to end the conversation.

**When you're listening in a conversation.** Sometimes pausing is a good way to stop you from giving the wrong response. It can prevent you from correcting, interrupting, or making a sarcastic remark. Give yourself permission to pause and think, *Am I truly listening or just waiting for my turn to start talking again?*

**Before we say yes to a request.** Sometimes we make ourselves frantic by taking on too much work or too many projects. We need to learn to say no. Even if it's an assignment from a higher-up, we often have more bargaining room than we realize. We can ask for a deadline extension or even suggest another team member who might have more time or expertise.

**During a presentation.** You're focused on what you want to convey or cover, but can you stop for a few seconds to check in with your audience? It can be valuable to pause and ask, "Are you guys okay with what I'm saying? Is there anything you want to talk about right now? Can we take two minutes of quiet to write down any questions or comments for me?"

**In the middle of a task.** When you're busy working on a project, pause for a few moments and think, *What am I trying to do and why is it important? What does success look like?* In as little as ten seconds you could gain clarity and a renewed sense of purpose.

**During a crisis.** When everything is going sideways, it can be smart to pause. This is a chance to slow down, step away, think, and make a game plan so you can do the right next thing.

**In a moment of clarity.** You're having a big "aha" moment. You finally figured out a problem or had the breakthrough you've been working toward. Take a pause. What does this mean? What's next?

**In a moment of exhaustion.** It's the end of a long day (or week, or year). You gave your all and are depleted. If you keep going, you won't be able to do your best. Can you give yourself permission to pause?

**When you're feeling overwhelmed.** When nothing makes sense and you have no idea what to do, stop. Take a break. Call a time-out and pause. To keep going would only worsen your inner chaos.

**During a meeting.** Active collaboration can be draining, overwhelming, and stressful. Why not give the group a break? No phones, no conversation—just step away and pause. Then return refreshed and ready to get to work.

**In a moment of celebration.** Celebrations are a great time to enjoy the company of those you care about—your children, your spouse, your coworkers, and so on. When you're commemorating an anniversary, birthday, or other special event, why not stop and enjoy it?

**In a moment of achievement.** I give this advice to every business owner and entrepreneur I know: stop along the way to celebrate and experience your wins. Most people don't do this. Ten years can go by before you know it without you ever pausing to enjoy the ride. Whether it's your first win or just your most recent, take a pause to appreciate it.

**When you're going through a change or transition.** Maybe you're changing jobs. Maybe you're changing careers. Or you're going through a transition in your personal life. No matter the nature of the change, stop for quiet so you can contemplate and regroup. In retrospect, when I left my marketing job and started Sheffield in 2006, I should have taken some time to think and reflect. Starting a new job or a new company is very stressful, yet I didn't take a break. I jumped from one reality to another. I missed an opportunity to reflect. I missed a chance to set goals. I missed an opportunity to grieve. I strongly believe that people don't see the value in inserting a break between job or career changes. Of course, if you need to make money, start right away, but if you can, have a small vacation, retreat somewhere, assess your next move, get your mind right, and then make the move.

**While teaching someone something.** Great instructors and educators always build in breaks for their students to stop and think about the information they are learning. How can you build in pauses? Between exercises? At the beginning and end of instruction? In the middle of a lecture?

**In a decisive moment.** A big decision is on the horizon. Don't even think about moving ahead without a pause. Give yourself ample time to consider your options. Slow down. Be deliberate.

**In a day (or a week, month, year, or career).** I like to pause on Sundays to rest and recharge for the week ahead. We all have different needs; make sure to pause when it makes sense for you. And don't forget that people also pause mid-career for a sabbatical; you can also give yourself a brief hiatus when changing jobs.

To learn more, check out the *Just Saying* podcast, episode "Permission to Pause": podcast.thebrieflab.com/ep-230-permission -to-pause.

Are there other ways you can think of to pause in your life? At any given moment, you can press your "remote control" and give yourself permission to pause the action, the noise, the stress, and the obligation.

I allow for plenty of pauses in my day. Between meetings, before tasks, before and after the workday—there are endless ways to press pause and add more quiet to your life. Think of them—the way one of my coworkers does—as mental wardrobe changes. Pauses can always create a fresh start. We just have to be comfortable doing nothing.

## But Is It *Really* Okay to Do Nothing?

I'm a big fan of the television show *Seinfeld*. As you probably know, it's known as "a show about nothing." Jerry and the gang reliably turn the most mundane conversations and scenarios into comedic gold. It probably comes as no surprise that I too am all for doing nothing as a way to experience quiet. It's an extremely valuable tactic, because even when you're doing nothing, you're still doing *something*. And by the way, *Seinfeld*, while a show about nothing, still had plenty of plotlines and lots of action in every episode. (Who could forget when Jerry accidentally agreed to wear an ostentatious puffy shirt on national television? Or when the group spent an entire episode searching for their car in the parking deck?)

Seinfeld once said, "I am so busy doing nothing . . . that the idea of doing anything, which, as you know, always leads to something, cuts into the nothing and then forces me to have to drop everything."

Each day, we have the option to try and do everything, to try to do something, or to try to do nothing. Likewise, we can try to say everything, or say something, or say nothing. Which of these, do you think, is the hardest? You guessed it. Doing nothing is shockingly hard.

It takes discipline, decisiveness, and a choice to actually do nothing. In sports, when a person calls a time-out, a player may no longer be playing, but they are still doing something valuable; maybe it's recalibrating, adjusting, developing a new game plan, or thinking of their next move. Time-outs are important, even though they're not considered part of the action of the game.

Why shouldn't we take the same approach in the business world? When we act before we have thought carefully about our next move, we often regret it. When we fill every moment with busyness, we don't leave time for pauses that give us insights and clarity. Far better to spend more time "doing nothing" (which, again, is really something) than spin our wheels and get very little done.

## Asking Someone to Give You Autonomy

You may be in complete agreement with everything I have said until now (which would be great!). Yet you may be thinking, *My boss, coworkers, or clients won't let me stop. During the day, I want to step away, yet they want to pull me in even closer.* It may be 4 PM on a Thursday afternoon, and I have scheduled some downtime to plan for next week, review the past few days, or read a journal to hone my craft. And then someone stops by, or a client calls with an urgent request. Or I hear and see a text notification with a quick request.

I want to give myself permission to pause, but what do I do if they won't let me? It's a fair question and real concern.

Here are a few things I would do to gain some autonomy—that is, the authority and ability to make the call without someone pulling it away from me unexpectedly or unfairly:

- **Act like you have autonomy (until someone says you don't).** In many cases, professionals think that they don't have the authority to go off the grid, step away, or work alone away from the team. In reality, they have already given up. What often works is to act like someone has said it's okay, and then wait to see if anyone challenges it or calls you out. If they do, fine. If they don't, you may already have the green light to get some quiet work done.

- **Have a real conversation about expectations.** Setting expectations often requires talking openly about them versus making assumptions. If doing quiet work is essential to getting your job done and your boss or coworkers are continually disrupting you from doing it, then it is probably time to sit down with them and talk about what works for you and what doesn't, and for them to do the same. You may find that simply publishing a daily schedule from 4 to 5 PM as your quiet work window might be enough for them to know to leave you alone. Remember: people aren't mind readers, so tell them what you need.

- **Set some clear, defensible boundaries.** Everyone has a need for quiet time, but the way it's established may differ from person to person. Setting boundaries may be establishing time slots that are off-limits, or putting a simple sign on your desk, or wearing headphones. Whatever line you draw, you get to establish a boundary that protects you.

- **Push back gently (or forcefully) when lines cross.** Initially, people who abuse your focus time may not even notice they are doing it, or care very much that it happens. Not surprisingly, you'll have to feel the effects of their crises and chaos along with them. When they do not respect or follow your suggested limit, you should say something to remind them. It may be a gentle reminder at first, and it may escalate to having a tough conversation about your need for quiet competing with their incessant need to interrupt, disrupt, or distract.

Autonomy is empowering, yet not everyone thinks they have it. To protect yourself and give yourself permission to pause, you may need to ask someone else if it's okay. Assume people are reasonable until they turn out not to be.

## A Few Scenarios Where Nothing Can Be Something

Below are some situations I want you to try on. I'm going to describe scenarios where one is likely to stay active out of habit or impulse. But in each scenario there lies a rich opportunity to choose to do nothing. Use these to practice getting into the mindset of nothingness (even though it's always somethingness).

**Scenario #1. A day filled with meetings.** You're in the office and have a thirty-minute break between meetings. How are you going to fill that half hour? Do you jump on your computer and start sending emails? Do you refer to your to-do list and check off a few tasks? How hard would it be to spend just fifteen minutes doing nothing? How would you feel if you simply stopped?

**Scenario #2. A few minutes before takeoff.** You're at the airport with about ten minutes until your flight boards. You look around and notice that everyone around you is on their phones. What will you do next? What if you spent the next ten minutes doing nothing? Could you simply let your mind wander?

**Scenario #3. It's a brand-new day.** It's 8 AM and you're working from home. Your workday has just begun. How do you start your morning? Do you turn on technology and get connected with your coworkers? Or do you spend the first half hour of your day doing nothing?

To learn more, check out the *Just Saying* podcast, episode "The Discipline of Doing Nothing": podcast.thebrieflab.com/ep-275-the-discipline-of-doing-nothing.

It is super easy to find something to do to fill those pockets of time we all get now and then. You might look at your phone, get on Slack, check email, do some busywork, go through your to-dos. But should you? No. Take time to pause. Build the discipline to do nothing, and you will always have it available as a tool you can use to discover your next insight, plan, or breakthrough.

Remember that we were built for breaks. We weren't meant to go, go, go nonstop. We were meant to take days off, to go on vacation, and to slow down sometimes without any guilt. We must model the same kind of rhythms in our professional lives. We can't afford not to, because quiet moments give our minds the breaks that bring about inspiration and breakthroughs.

Case in point: there's a great book called *Bored and Brilliant: How Spacing Out Can Unlock Your Most Productive and Creative Self.* It turns out that the ability to push through those moments when you have nothing to do and feel bored is the source of innovation, creativity, analysis, and purpose. For many people, being bored means instinctively, impulsively jumping on their smartphone or turning on the television to do something, anything, whether it's productive, amusing, or just something to keep away total boredom. I tend to do this while sitting at a stoplight or waiting in line—any time there are pockets of waiting. It's like eating when you're bored: we feed on our devices to fill the boredom. Not only is this an enormous source of noise for people, but it is also a lost opportunity. Now I try to be conscious of this habit, this manifestation to look at my phone during these moments, and place it face down so I can be comfortable and present and simply let my mind wander. That's why you hear people saying they have some of their best ideas in the shower. In fact, I had a client who called his bathroom muse "Mr. Moen," referring to the faucet manufacturer!

That's why I challenge you to sometimes do nothing. To say nothing. And to think about nothing.

Not for nothing; indeed, quiet is the gateway to everything.

## BRIEFLY STATED

Make sure that chaos doesn't drive you. Develop the discipline to do nothing and give yourself permission to pause.

## QUIET CONSIDERATIONS

**DO I:** fall into the trap of filling every waking moment with technology or other distractions?

**WOULD I:** be more intentional, more focused, and more directed if I gave myself permission to pause at crucial, or even non-crucial, moments during the day?

**CAN I:** give myself grace and accept the permission to intentionally pause once, then twice, then more each day?

# Chapter 11

# Leave Me Alone—It Can Wait! (Not Everything Is an Emergency)

A few years ago, I was driving to my brother's house to pick something up that I had loaned him. On the way, I kept trying to get in touch with my nephew to make sure he would be home when I arrived. I called him over and over and even left a message. By this point I was starting to get agitated. I kept thinking, *Why is he not picking up?!* He did call me back after about twenty-five minutes, but by then I had changed my plans. It wasn't the end of the world, but in the moment, it was upsetting, and it ruined my afternoon.

Why did this missed connection bother me so much? I can now see that I was angered by my unfulfilled expectation. It's human nature. We expect things in life to happen in a specific way, and when things don't work out the way we planned, we get mad, frustrated, and discouraged. In this case, my irritation stemmed from having to wait.

Following the incident with my nephew, I started reflecting on why we expect everything to happen immediately—and how that expectation is making our lives worse.

## The Illusion of Immediacy

Our world has changed so much in just a few years. Things that used to take a long time happen quickly now. Years ago, when I lived in Spain, calling home was so expensive that I had to write letters to stay in touch with my family. It could take weeks for a single letter to reach home. How things have changed! Today I can email, FaceTime, or text friends or loved ones from anywhere in the world. If I want to learn about a new subject, I don't have to go to the library and search the card catalog; I can just google it and get an answer in seconds. If I need to get from point A to point B, I don't have to pull out a map and chart a course. GPS or Waze will get me there—and show me the fastest routes.

These advances haven't just changed our lives; they've changed our expectations. We expect to have access to anything in no time flat. We feel entitled to immediacy. If we send a text or email, we expect an instant reply. When we want information, we expect it *yesterday*.

Here's the thing, though: the expectation of immediacy is an illusion. We *can't* have everything the moment we want it. We've bought into this false belief, and it is negatively impacting our relationships, extending all the way to our daily interactions with our colleagues in the workplace.

We work in the era of instant, urgent, now, now, now! People feel entitled to talk to us or receive a response the minute they want it. On a whim they can call, email, or text us, or even walk over to our workstation—and often we feel obligated to stop what we are doing and converse.

And it goes both ways. Think about the last time you tried reaching out to someone who did not respond right away. If you wondered why they weren't standing by, waiting for your call or email, you're in good company.

To learn more, check out the *Just Saying* podcast, episode "The Illusion of Immediacy": podcast.thebrieflab.com/episode-80 -the-illusion-of-immediacy.

The expectation of immediacy is more than a mere frustration for professionals. It destroys our ability to focus and perform. When you're in the flow of thinking, planning, or writing, the last thing you need is an uninvited interruption. Yet the workplace is full of disruptions because we all collectively operate as if *everything is due in five minutes.* Even if you manage to carve out some time for quiet, you're likely to be interrupted, because ...

## We Treat Everything like an Emergency!

Yes, we all do this. Everything feels heightened and urgent. Further, we are so used to getting whatever we want immediately that we adopt the belief that we (along with everyone else) must always be on the grid. We are afraid to step away from the computer, or our work email, or our phones, because someone might send us an email or text that can't wait. What if someone stops by our cubicle and we've stepped away for an hour of quiet? Surely the world would end!

Not really. Even if we might feel like every call, every Slack message, every text demands an immediate response, most things aren't emergencies. Everything can't be hot all at once. And if you treat everything as an emergency, you can never prioritize tasks. Things that are urgent but not important will overwhelm you and steal your attention span.

The bottom line: unless you're an actual 911 dispatcher, chances are you can step away for some quiet without dire consequences. Many, if not most, things *can* wait.

When you accept this truth, it empowers you to take the quiet time you need to be your best. It allows others to do this for themselves as well.

But adopting this mindset isn't easy. Many people and organizations have a scarcity mentality that can impact the way they approach work. We believe there isn't enough—enough business, enough money, and, most of all, enough *time*—and that belief drives our sense of urgency. (To be fair, the uncertain world we live in could make anyone jumpy!) Further, employees—especially those without as much experience—may err on the side of sharing too much information with their leaders out of caution.

I believe we can find the right balance that keeps us in the loop and allows us to receive pertinent information without being in constant contact. After all, good leaders empower people to take ownership of their work and trust them to do their jobs independently. They don't micromanage or handhold. And they train employees to know when to connect about critical information and when it's okay to send a message, trusting that you'll reply when you're ready.

## *No, Not Now*: Three Small but Powerful Words to Lower the Volume

*No* is a word that's overlooked a lot in the workplace. But it exerts a tremendous amount of power. At a time when the lines blur between our roles—professional, parent, partner, volunteer—we need *no* more than ever to lower the volume, tighten our focus, and strengthen our attention.

Distractions and disruptions come all the time, and *no* can help shift you back into focus. Let's say, for example, you're working—writing an email—and you get a text or a Slack message and the distraction comes. That might be a moment where you could say, "No. Not now." *No* can seem like a very permanent thing, but it is simply

"No. Not now." You are giving yourself permission to gracefully push the distraction away until later. You buy yourself some time, acknowledging that their sense of urgency is different from yours.

*No* sounds definitively negative or forever, but it doesn't mean that you cannot or will not ever circle back to acknowledge the distraction. *No* simply means that right now you choose to focus on something else. In doing this, you are saying *yes* to quiet. You are saying *yes* to focus. You are saying *yes* to something else.

To learn more, check out the *Just Saying* podcast, episode "Saying No, Not Now": podcast.thebrieflab.com/episode-137-saying -no-not-now.

## A Method to Control the Madness

That said, it is useful to set some parameters to guide your coworkers or employees on when to get in touch and when something can wait. The US military has addressed this very issue.

I consult with military clients who routinely must make important, often critical decisions. But even these aren't always treated as emergencies. Military leaders are trained to determine the urgency of the information they receive and how it needs to be delivered. They use what is known as the Commanders Critical Information Requirements (CCIR) to make these kinds of calls. The CCIR lays out the criteria that make information so important it warrants waking the commander in the middle of the night or pulling them out of a meeting. With clear guidance in place, people understand what is and isn't an emergency, and therefore they have a firm grasp on how to communicate. It works for the military, and it can work for the rest of us, too.

There are other tools that give similar guidance for professionals. Stephen Covey's Time Management Matrix is one such tool. The Time Management Matrix consists of four quadrants you can use to prioritize your professional tasks. It is strikingly similar to another tool for managing high-stakes issues, the Eisenhower Matrix, named after Dwight D. himself. While Covey's matrix focuses on time spent on task and the Eisenhower Matrix represents the tasks themselves, they essentially do the same thing: help you decide what needs your time and attention and what can wait. *Remember, unless you are a 911 dispatcher, very little of what you do each day is a true emergency.*

**Quadrant I: Urgent and Important**
*Something that needs to be done right away. Do it now.*

- A key member of the leadership team has unexpectedly quit right in the middle of the biggest project of the year, and you need to meet to discuss the organization's next steps.

**Quadrant II: Not Urgent but Important**
*Something that must happen soon but is not an emergency. Put it on your calendar.*

- You need to draw up a budget, but you have until the end of the month to get it done.

**Quadrant III: Urgent but Not Important**
*Something that can wait or be delegated to another person.*

- Your supervisor has requested a status report on the project you're leading.

**Quadrant IV: Not Urgent and Not Important**
*Something that you don't need to deal with now ... or perhaps ever.*

- Your spam folder is overflowing with junk mail.

You can use this matrix to figure out what belongs in each quadrant in your world.

**Take a step back and assess your actions.** Look at your own behavior throughout your professional day. How do you make yourself available to other people? How do you manage your responsibilities and tasks? **Once you've done this, make a conscious mind shift toward a new approach.** You need to be able to say with confidence, "Leave me alone; it can wait." Because many things, in fact, can wait.

## Seven Steps to Curb the Emergencies and Make Space for Quiet

Now that you are able to determine which tasks are urgent and important, you can start helping your team align with your preferences and ultimately create time and space for more quiet in your professional life. Follow these steps:

1.  **Discuss with your team what constitutes an emergency and warrants an immediate interruption.** Remember, these criteria are relative to your life and work. If you're working in a very important leadership role, you might have a totally different definition of what constitutes an emergency than a different employee would.
2.  **Define what is important and what is urgent.** Share the parameters that make something urgent. Then do the same for determining what's important.

3. **Discuss appropriate time windows.** If you're asking people to either contact you right away or wait, it's important to figure out what constitutes timeliness and what constitutes waiting. Because if you're telling people, "Leave me alone; it can wait," you need to be able to define what "waiting" is. Maybe it's fifteen minutes. Maybe it's an hour, or four hours. Maybe it's a day or a week. Be specific.

4. **Share the best way to reach you.** Rank your preferred methods of communication. A phone call might not be the best option for you. Maybe you prefer a text instead. After a text, you might prefer a Slack message or an instant message on the corporate system. Then an email, then a meeting. Then share your preferences with others so they can respect these boundaries.

5. **Establish your emergency contact.** Just to be safe, have one person who knows how to get a hold of you during your quiet time. Make sure they understand that they should only reach out in a true emergency.

6. **Disconnect (entirely) and enjoy your quiet time.** Once these parameters are clear with your team or colleagues, disconnect completely. You're off the grid for however long you choose.

7. **Debrief with your team or colleagues.** Is the system working? Do you need to adjust? Does the team accept your boundaries?

To learn more, check out the *Just Saying* podcast, episode "Leave Me Alone, It Can Wait!": podcast.thebrieflab.com/ep-294-leave-me-alone-it-can-wait.

The idea of saying, "Leave me alone; it can wait" may seem selfish to you at first. I assure you it is not. If you don't get this part right, you'll always have to be "on," and everything will be an emergency. This means a career in which you can't focus, plan, or disconnect.

You deserve better, and so does everyone else. If you get this right, you can disconnect and say with confidence, "No, not now." And you can take the quiet you need. Here's hoping the real emergencies in your future are few and far between.

## BRIEFLY STATED

Not everything is an emergency, so we need to shed the illusion of immediacy, learn how to create spaces for quiet, and remember that most things can wait.

## QUIET CONSIDERATIONS

**DO I**: feel frustration when immediate responses are expected but not delivered?

**WOULD I**: be able to prioritize my professional tasks, disconnect, and empower my employees to do the same?

**CAN I**: think of a moment when I felt I couldn't turn off my computer for fear of being seen as unavailable?

## Chapter 12

# The Quiet Works Toolkit: Six Ways to Make Quiet Time Stick

Q uiet is a simple concept that creates powerful change. (If you don't know this by now, I haven't done my job well!) But we all know *simple* isn't always synonymous with *easy*. The reality is, it can be challenging to build blocks of quiet into your professional life in a way that will stick.

Practicing quiet is solitary work. It's easy to give up when there's no one holding you accountable or when you work all day as a collaborative worker. That's why it's useful to have a few go-to tools to help you stay committed and make quiet an integral part of your day.

In this chapter I am sharing a series of very practical—and highly effective—resources I have introduced to help you build quiet into your day. I have developed these over the years to offer you several ways to approach quiet time. Having a variety of options staves off frustration and resignation and keeps you coming back to your practice.

Let's jump right in.

# Tool #1: A Quiet Quiz to Gauge
# Your Strengths and Weaknesses

How noisy is your work environment? Most of our days are so filled with distractions and disruptions that it's difficult to concentrate or get things done. This shouldn't be the norm, but it's the reality for many organizations. To see how you and your work environment measure up, take the Quiet Works™ Quiet Quiz by visiting quietworkplace.scoreapp.com. The quiz gauges the following four categories:

- Information consumption
- Distractions and disruptions
- Time for quiet
- Places for quiet

Your results may or may not surprise you. But either way they will give you a good starting point and a thoughtful idea of the obstacles keeping you from performing at a higher level.

Encourage your team to take the quiz as well. You can discuss the results, raise awareness around the impact of noise, and start thinking of solutions together.

## Tool #2: The Lineup to Create a Daily Plan to Win

When I was writing the book *NOISE*, I kept thinking about noise as our enemy, our constant competitor, our nemesis. It wants to take us down through distraction and disruption, and we need a game plan to defeat it. Because if we don't beat noise, it's going to beat us.

Now, I love sports, but we can all appreciate the comparison between game day and the workday. In sports, the manager or coach puts together a lineup of who is playing that day. You've got your regular players and your specialty players. Daily players are always in the lineup. In soccer, you'll always have a goalie; in American football, a quarterback; in baseball, a pitcher. But sometimes you might field certain players against more challenging opponents or move players around based on certain situations: an attacking midfielder, more linebackers, or a left-handed pitcher. These are the specialty players, and even though they're not always needed on the field or court for every game, they are equally essential if you want to win.

It's the same with planning your workday. You need a lineup of proven tactics to help you be at your most creative, energetic, and productive. The Lineup is your game plan that guarantees success.

You can chart out your lineup each day when you start work. It can even be a part of your morning quiet time. Here's a quick overview of what the Lineup looks like:

### *"Daily Players" (always in the lineup)*

**First Thought.** This is your headline to start the day. It should be intentional, as it sets the tone for everything else. It could highlight an important goal or set an intention, such as "I *will not* sweat the little stuff" or "I'm focusing on just today."

**Quiet Time—AM.** Plan for and schedule morning quiet time. Remember, it's a nonnegotiable appointment that sets the tone for the day.

# { The Lineup™ }

## DAILY PLAYERS ► Role Details

**Daily Players are needed to compete every day.** Their planned presence and performance are essential to consistently defeat the noise day to day.

| Daily Player | Notes |
|---|---|
| ☐ **First Thought** <br> Headline to start your day | |
| ☐ **Quiet Time–AM** <br> Moments just for your thoughts | |
| ☐ **Read Time** <br> Tackle your reading list | |
| ☐ **The Big Moment** <br> What matters most in the day | |
| ☐ **Daily Scan** <br> Looking ahead and behind | |
| ☐ **Quiet Time–PM** <br> Moments just for your thoughts | |
| ☐ **Final Thought** <br> Headline that wraps up your day | |

## SPECIALTY PLAYERS ► Role Details

**Specialty Players give you options to adjust your ongoing game plan.** Their presence gives you unique ways to focus on winning moment to moment, day to day.

| Specialty Player | Notes |
|---|---|
| ☐ **Presence of Mind** <br> Thinking about your thinking | |
| ☐ **Rhythm of Repetition** <br> Using words & phrases to focus | |
| ☐ **Mute More Often** <br> Say no to devices & distractions | |
| ☐ **Take 5** <br> Focus on one thing for 5 minutes | |
| ☐ **Present Listening** <br> The quality of your listening | |
| ☐ **Brevity** <br> Communicating clearly & concisely | |
| ☐ **Other** <br> Alternate ways to manage noise | |

**Read Time.** Time spent reading up on your craft (even just five minutes) is never time wasted.

**The Big Moment.** This is the most important part of your day. Maybe it's a meeting. Maybe it's a deadline. Know what it is and approach it with utmost attention.

**Daily Scan.** Take a few minutes to review your day. What's coming up next? What's already happened? How's it going?

**Quiet Time—PM.** This is the hardest afternoon appointment to keep. Stick to it no matter what.

**Final Thought.** Reflect on the day. How did it go? Then go to sleep (without your smartphone nearby).

### *"Specialty Players" (use when special occasions/opponents arise)*

**Presence of Mind.** Ask yourself: Where's my head at today? Am I focused on the small details, or the big picture, or something else? You may need to remind yourself of one key thought (e.g., be deliberate, finish a task, take notes).

**Rhythm of Repetition.** These are mantras or words to help you focus. Maybe: *Slow down. Be kind. One thing at a time.* Say these to yourself—and write them down.

**Mute More Often.** Here's your reminder to say no more often during your day. Mute your devices. Tune out distractions. Frequently, you may need to say, "No, not now."

**Take 5.** Schedule a short break during the day. Recenter. Prepare five minutes before a call or take five after one for notes. This can be a tech time-out, staying off social media, or ignoring self-induced distractions.

**Present Listening.** Give others your full attention when they speak. If you catch yourself planning what you will say next or getting distracted by other thoughts, refocus on the conversation.

**Brevity.** These are your daily insights and reminders to be clear and concise. Write down words or phrases that are short, sweet, and to the point.

**Other.** This is where you can identify alternate ways to reduce and manage noise—lessons you learned from others or insights you gained through thoughtful reflection.

### What's Most Important Today?

Finally, the Lineup helps you answer the question, **"What's Most Important?"** We all wear a lot of hats: manager, parent, leader, volunteer, friend, sibling, etc. Some days it's most important to be a dad, a boss, or a brother. Other days your role as an executive or volunteer might be critical. Each day, you can list your core focus by role to help you stay centered on what matters most. This helps lower the noise and needs to be done during your quiet time.

- Fill out this simple sentence: *In my role as* _____, *the most important thing today is* _____.
- Do it again: *In my role as* _____, *the most important thing to-day is* _____."
- Do it again: *In my role as* _____, *the most important thing today is* _____."

# [ Today ]

Date:

☐☐ - ☐☐ - ☐☐
M   T   W   TH   F   SA   SU

## PRIORITIES ► What's Most Important?

In my role as: _____
the most important thing today is

_____

In my role as: _____
the most important thing today is

_____

In my role as: _____
the most important thing today is

_____

In my role as: _____
the most important thing today is

_____

## SCHEDULE

6a _____

7a _____

8a _____

9a _____

10a _____

11a _____

12p _____

1p _____

2p _____

3p _____

4p _____

5p _____

6p _____

7p _____

8p _____

## TO DO LIST

☐ _____

☐ _____

☐ _____

☐ _____

☐ _____

☐ _____

☐ _____

☐ _____

☐ _____

☐ _____

☐ _____

☐ _____

☐ _____

☐ _____

☐ _____

## NOTES

Over the past few years, filling out this simple sentence during times of quiet, either in the morning for the day ahead or in the afternoon for the day to come, has been so rewarding to me. At times it is simple. Other times, it is more difficult. I try to make it specific and actionable—and often something small. Doing this every day will make a huge difference in being intentional.

We are often hopeful that we will be able to manage noise on the fly, but that rarely happens. Without a plan, you'll succumb to noise and your day, week, year, or even your career will be a blur. That's the hamster-wheel effect, and it happens to well-meaning professionals every day. You may choose not to follow this specific Lineup model and instead have some other kind of daily plan. Use your chosen method to organize your workday. You'll be glad you did.

> To learn more, check out the *Just Saying* podcast, episode "The Lineup": podcast.thebrieflab.com/episode-171-the-lineup.

## Tool #3: A Sign That Shows Them You Mean (Quiet) Business

Much like signage requesting quiet in a library or the Do Not Disturb message hanging on a hotel door, a physical sign can let your coworkers know the times you'd like to be left alone. It's a great, low-tech way to get your point across clearly (and nicely). Remember that people are not mind readers—and that quiet is *invisible* work done alone. Without something in place to alert them that you don't want to be disturbed, they will assume you are open for business.

**To purchase a Do Not Disturb sign, please visit thequietworkplace.com.**

Signs are especially important in open floor plan–style offices, which are common in many organizations. With no door to close, how can people know you'd like to be left alone? A sign sends the message and spares you from interruption. So post one on your cubicle wall, hang it from your computer monitor, or place it on the edge of your desk. No one likes to interrupt others, so people will appreciate the heads-up.

Amazon, for instance, has no official nor corporate Amazon culture sign that indicates "do not disturb." Individuals have to find their own nook for quiet. However, at one site, a person took the initiative to put up a "Meeting in Session" sign requesting quiet and no interruptions. This has now become a standard practice at that site.

Your Do Not Disturb sign doesn't need to be fancy. One manager at Coca-Cola simply switched from wearing a green Coca-Cola hat to a red one when he didn't want to be disturbed. Even a Post-it note will nicely convey the message that you're unavailable.

Even if you don't use a physical sign with words like "do not disturb," there are other ways to express your need for quiet. For example: noise-canceling headphones, earplugs or earbuds, and closing your door (if you have one). You can even find "busy lights" online that glow in different colors to show others when you're available and when you're not.

Further, there are several options for digital Do Not Disturb signs. Platforms like Slack and Teams have symbols that alert online interrupters that you are in a meeting or in deep thought so they won't disturb you.

Here are some instructions for setting up DNDs on some popular work management platforms:

- In Slack, click your profile picture in the top right, hover over **pause notifications**, and choose a time from the menu or **select custom** to set your own.
- In Microsoft Outlook, select **File** > **Options** > **Mail**, and under **Message Arrival**, select or clear the **Display a Desktop Alert** checkbox and then select **OK**.
- In Microsoft Teams, if you want to make sure people know when you're *busy* or *away* from your desk, set your status in Teams. The little dot on your profile indicates if you're available or not.

Go to your profile at the top of Teams and select one from the list. You can also update your status from the command box. Type **/available, /busy, /dnd, /brb, /away,** or **/offline** to set your status as *Available, Busy, Do Not Disturb, Be Right Back, Away,* or *Offline.*

There are also several ways to set Do Not Disturbs on our cell phones:

**For iPhone:** The Focus feature on your iPhone helps you tune out distractions during work or other activities. For example, a work Focus silences notifications from all people and apps except those you choose to hear from.

- To set up a work Focus, go to **Settings** > **Focus** and choose the **Work** option. Then, choose the people (or apps) that you would like to hear from, if any, while in Work mode.
- From there, you can choose to show any silenced notifications on your Lock Screen, to darken your lock screen, or to hide notification badges.
- The Focus function is highly customizable. You can select a Smart Activation that turns on Focus automatically at certain times, locations, or even while using a certain app. And to silence all notifications quickly, go to **Control Center** > **Focus** > **Do Not Disturb.**

**For Android:** If you're an Android user, you can silence your phone (muting sounds, stopping vibration, and blocking visual disturbances) with Android's Do Not Disturb function.

- To turn on Do Not Disturb quickly, swipe down from the top of your screen and tap **Do Not Disturb.**
- Android allows you to choose what/who you would like to block

during Do Not Disturb. To establish your preferred settings, select **Sound** > **Do Not Disturb**. Under "What can interrupt Do Not Disturb," choose from **People, Apps,** or **Alarms and other interruptions** to customize your preferences.

- Additionally, you can turn on Do Not Disturb automatically during events and meetings on your Google Calendar, or at certain times throughout the day.

One more thing to keep in mind about Do Not Disturbs: before putting up a sign (of any kind), have a chat with your coworkers to let them know you'll need occasional quiet time. It could go something like this: "Hey, I'm going to be taking some quiet time each day, and I don't want to be disturbed. If you see this sign on my desk, please come back later. Thank you so much."

Not only is a physical or digital sign useful during your quiet time, but it can also make a tremendous difference throughout the day. Much of what we do at work requires undisturbed focus, such as composing an email, thinking through what you'll say in a meeting, or preparing a presentation. So show your sign, and enjoy uninterrupted quiet and focus.

> To learn more, check out the *Just Saying* podcast, episode "Give Me a Sign (Do Not Disturb): podcast.thebrieflab.com/ep-250-give-me-a-sign-do-not-disturb.

## Tool #4: Take-5 Quiet Cards to Give You a Choice

I was inspired to create the Take 5 Cards™ deck during a very busy, hectic time in my life. I would carve out little pockets here and there for quiet, but then I would often discover that I had no idea how to spend that time. Finally, I thought, *Wouldn't it be great if I had cards with a variety of suggested activities that I could do?* So I wrote an A-to-Z selection of things I could do in as little as five minutes.

Suddenly I had real choices and valuable options, not just my mind racing in a dozen different directions. And now so will you. If you're unsure of how to spend your quiet, just pick a card, any card. The element of surprise bolsters your creativity and may lead you to some unexpected places.

When I created the Take 5 Cards, I imagined categories of things that I would be able to do for five minutes. When I was done, I could continue for another five minutes doing the same thing or grab another card. For me, there were initially several categories that were appealing: planning, reading, and writing. Surprisingly, two categories emerged that helped me greatly: thanking and nothing. The gratitude card gave me time to consider all the things that were positive in my life, career, and relationships. And the nothing card gave my brain time to slow down and cool off. I was inspired to create these cards during scheduled quiet time, ironically.

Here's a brief example of some of the categories:

I use this quiet time to recognize a personal circumstance, challenge, condition, position or situation.

## ACCEPTING

IN OTHER WORDS:
receive, take, admit, consent, agree, assent, undertake, acknowledge, assume.

---

I use this quiet time to freely decide on a course of action, thought, feeling or attitude.

## CHOOSING

IN OTHER WORDS:
to select, pick, take, indicate, elect, decide, want, prefer, favor.

---

I use this quiet time to bemoan someone or something that may impact me adversely.

## COMPLAINING

IN OTHER WORDS:
to protest, criticize, grumble, nitpick, whine, moan, murmur.

---

I use this quiet time to let my heart and mind yearn for something special.

## DREAMING

IN OTHER WORDS:
to imagine, envision, wish, desire, picture, aspire, visualize.

---

I use this quiet time to enjoy something present before me (e.g., thought, feeling, action, condition, etc.).

## ENJOYING

IN OTHER WORDS:
to appreciate, like, love, relish, experience.

---

I use this quiet time to pay close attention to the sounds all around me.

## LISTENING

IN OTHER WORDS:
to notice, detect, discover, identify, distinguish, perceive all the different noises that surround me in the moment.

I use this quiet time to express my gratitude.

**THANKING**

IN OTHER WORDS:
to appreciate, recognize, accept, value, grasp, acknowledge.

I use this quiet time for contemplation.

**THINKING**

IN OTHER WORDS:
to consider, wonder, reason, plan, ponder, ruminate, reflect, deliberate, meditate.

I use this quiet time to turn my thoughts into words.

**WRITING**

IN OTHER WORDS:
to create, compose, edit, draft, revise.

I use this quiet time to determine possible approaches or courses of action.

**PLANNING**

IN OTHER WORDS:
to design, plot, strategize, solve, resolve, propose, suggest, scheme.

I use this quiet time to read.

**READING**

IN OTHER WORDS:
to read a book, notes, poetry, essay, speech, article, lyrics.

I use this quiet time to not do anything.

**NOTHING**

IN OTHER WORDS:
zero, zip, nil, naught, zilch.

I soon realized that five minutes was the perfect amount of time for the activities on the cards (an hour divides nicely and evenly by five-minute blocks). When you receive an unexpected gift of time—like when a meeting ends a few minutes early—you can use those minutes to Prepare or Choose or Read. If you have more time, you can grab multiple cards and do several quiet activities. (For example, in a sixty-minute window of time, you can do twelve five-minute sessions. If you have thirty minutes for quiet, you can choose six five-minute activities, and so on.)

To learn more, check out the *Just Saying* podcast, episode "Take 5 Quiet Cards": podcast.thebrieflab.com/episode-167 -take-5-quiet-cards.
To purchase a set of Take 5 Cards, please visit thequietworkplace.com.

## Zero In: One Thing at a Time

Quiet is about lowering your noise levels, not increasing them. So no matter which action or prompt you choose to do, it's important to do only one at a time. No multitasking allowed. Attempting to do ten (or even two!) things at once will make you stressed and anxious and negate the very benefits you want to gain. Studies show that our brain simply isn't capable of paying full attention to more than one thing. For example, Dr. David Meyer and Dr. Joshua Rubinstein conducted research concluding that "brief mental blocks that happen as a result of context switching cost as much as 40% of someone's productive time."[1] Another research study at the University of California at Irvine found that, on average, it takes around twenty-three minutes for most workers to get back on task after an interruption.[2]

If you're going to spend your quiet cleaning, just clean. If you're going to rest, just rest. If you're going to think, just think.

## Tool #5: A Notebook That Makes a Pen and Paper Powerful

# Notes

# Notes

*The quieter you become the more you are able to hear.*

—RUMI

A simple notebook is an invaluable tool during your quiet time or any other time. What better way to capture your thoughts whenever they come? Without the distractions of technology, you'll be amazed by your insights and reflections. You might prefer to think of it as journaling, or you might not. The process can be structured, in which you write according to a prompt, or a stream of consciousness—letting your mind just wander. There's something about putting pen to paper that fuels the creative process.

I wasn't in the habit of doing this. After taking notes in college, I stopped doing it as an adult. But when I started scheduling quiet time for myself, I brought a notebook into my quiet-time appointments and began to jot down my thoughts. If the pages were empty, that was okay. I didn't have to write anything down, but when I did, I would scribble down my thoughts, both professional and personal. I discovered it was very beneficial to go back and reread my notes and reflect on them. It gives you a sense of your thinking, your growth, and even if there are blank pages, it makes one consider, *What was I thinking or doing on this day?* or *How have I changed since then?*

A modest notebook is a low-tech game changer. Choose the style that suits your needs, whether lined, gridded, or blank. Carry one with you wherever you go. If you prefer, you can even keep several categorized notebooks for business use, personal use, creative use, etc. The Quiet Works™ Notebook features both lined sheets and gridded sheets suitable for multiple uses.

> **To purchase a QuietWorks™ Notebook, please visit**
> **thequietworkplace.com.**

## TOOL #6: Toys and Games to Relax and Reset ("Playtime" for Professionals)

Everyone gets a little anxious from time to time. For those moments, some relaxing play can be very beneficial. Find a toy or game to keep your hands busy and your mind calm. Squeeze a stress ball or play with a fidget spinner. Play a game of solitaire. Color or work on a Rubik's Cube. You might notice these are all low-tech suggestions. It's better to relax with a physical object like a fidget spinner or coloring book than to play a game on your phone or computer—since that is likely to tempt you to check your email or social media account. Staying low tech helps you avoid that rabbit hole and spares you unnecessary noise, anxiety, and distraction.

——————

Use these tools every day. They are small but mighty and will help cut through the chaos and filter out the noise. Every tool in your toolkit makes a difference. And, little by little, they will bring you closer to the quiet you crave.

## BRIEFLY STATED

We often need practical tools to help us get started with establishing quiet practices. These tools demystify our attempts and create the best odds for success.

## QUIET CONSIDERATIONS

**DO I:** have clearly established strategies that communicate—to my colleagues and coworkers—my need for quiet during the workday?

**WOULD I:** be able to utilize the Lineup tactically to help diminish the craziness of my daily schedule and peel away the layers of noise?

**CAN I:** not only encourage my team to recognize the importance of quiet time but also ask them to examine the work environment and create solutions to raise awareness on the need for quiet?

# Chapter 13

# Tech Time-Outs
# to Reclaim Your Day

Who hasn't fallen down a tech-induced rabbit hole? I certainly have many times. It starts by glancing at my phone to check the time. Then I look at my email, then a website, some social media, a few sports scores, then LinkedIn. Before I know it, I'm far down a path I hadn't intended to take. It's a journey that takes lots of time and is rarely rewarding.

I'm not alone. In fact, the research is very clear that most of us struggle to detach from technology. It's what makes quiet so hard, because it's so inviting and addictive. Here's the world we live in and from which we can't detach:

- **Most people now have smartphones.** A Digital 2023 Global Overview Report shows 5.44 billion people, or almost 70 percent of the world population, have a cell phone.[1]
- **We are constantly connected to technology.** Internet users ages sixteen to sixty-four surf the internet approximately 6.5 hours,

broadcast and stream TV about 3.5 hours, and use social media just over two hours per day.[2]

- **There's diverse and dominant digital device ownership.** From teens to adults, 96.2 own a mobile phone, 95.6 percent own a smartphone, 58 percent own a desktop or laptop computer, 33.7 percent own a tablet, 29.9 percent own a smart watch, and 5.6 percent own a virtual reality device.[3]
- **We're stuck on Slack during weekdays and weekends.** A 2019 Slack post reports that the average time users are connected to Slack per workday is around nine hours. In addition, they spend approximately ninety minutes per workday actively using Slack.[4]
- **Screens in the household are multiplying.** A 2022 Statista article reports there are, on average, more than ten screens per household, with mobile phones, computers, and smart TVs being the top three.[5]
- **We have apps aplenty on our smartphones.** A 2021 SensorTower post cites that the average US mobile phone user used forty-six apps on average on their mobile devices.[6]
- **Heavy smartphone users swipe over four thousand times a day.**[7]
- **Our first and last daily contact is with tech.** In a survey conducted by The BRIEF Lab, 70 percent of respondents admitted to checking their phone first thing in the morning and as the last thing they did each day.[8]

It hasn't always been this way. Once upon a time (or even ten to twenty years ago), people communicated totally differently than they do now. If someone wasn't available by phone, you left a message with a service or on an answering machine. I know that way of life is long gone (and I don't miss it). Technology has made so many great things possible.

But technology has also created the immediacy that stifles us, which we touched on in chapter eleven. Just a few years ago, people were comfortable waiting a reasonable amount of time to correspond with their colleagues and business contacts. Professionals were allowed to be out of the office without dire consequences. And we all accepted that if someone was unavailable, they would get back in touch with us in a timely manner.

## The Unhealthy Impact of Technology

Today, we are all tethered to technology and succumb to it—even when we know it harms our career and our well-being. Career-wise, access to technology cuts both ways. On one hand, it can accelerate our work and help us communicate better. But we ignore the vast downside of "too much technology" at our peril. Taken to the extreme, it can hurt us personally, emotionally, and psychologically.

Problems can manifest in lots of different ways. Several years ago, I was leading a group through one of our BRIEF courses, and I mentioned the common phenomenon of a "phantom vibration," the feeling that your smartphone is vibrating or ringing when it's not, which is often linked to excessive phone use. When I mentioned it, someone in the class blurted out, "Thank you so much! I thought I was getting cancer because my I felt my leg vibrating and there was no phone, and I was going to see the doctor next week!" (He wasn't kidding.)

That's just one colorful example of the negative influence of technology. There are many other impacts as well.

In interpersonal relationships, overuse of tech can create strains between people. Beyond creating misunderstandings, it can cause a strong sense of jealousy, mistrust, and insecurity to see others more interested in being online than in a conversation. Fun fact: the habit of snubbing a physically present person for a smartphone is known as "phubbing."[9]

Being too attached to our devices drains the time we could spend with others and creates an emotional disconnect that takes a toll on the people in our lives as well as ourselves. A study at the University of Pennsylvania found that high usage of Facebook, Snapchat, and Instagram *increases* rather than decreases feelings of loneliness.[10] But loneliness is just the tip of the iceberg.

Overdependence on technology can also drastically impact our physical and mental health. It can lead to anxiety, depression, unhealthy expectations, concentration issues, and addiction. The research is significant and alarming in this area. According to a study by Common Sense Media, over a quarter of parents feel like they are addicted to their mobile phones.[11] Furthermore, smartphone and social media use correlates with symptoms of depression in younger people.[12]

Further, in a 2023 HelpGuide.org post, "Social Media and Mental Health," the authors state that "ironically for a technology that's designed to bring people closer together, spending too much time engaging with social media can actually make you feel more lonely and isolated." The article reports that "multiple studies have found a strong link between heavy social media and an increased risk for depression, anxiety, loneliness, self-harm, and even suicidal thoughts."[13]

For all of these reasons, it's important to schedule moments in the day when we are "off." This isn't a radical concept, either. Think of the stores that we all visit. They have open and closed hours, and we abide by them without question. There's no reason we shouldn't designate times when we are off the grid, guilt free. This is a powerful step toward building a healthier relationship with technology.

It's up to each of us to examine our habits and consider a digital diet. This will likely be challenging because using our smartphone (and other devices) is a deeply ingrained habit—and even an addiction—for most of us. You might even feel like you can't step away from technology, but that is a lie. You *can* work without technology. You and your thoughts are what you need, especially as we go further into a world of AI.

Always remember that your ability to think is what makes you uniquely human. Not the fact that you have a faster processor or the latest iOS. Your technology won't do the thinking for you. But it will drastically harm your quality of life if you allow it to dominate you all day and night.

Speaking of night, we also know that smartphones wreak havoc on our nightly rest. When numerous studies show using our phones at bedtime reduces the quality of our sleep as well as the quantity of it, you can't afford *not* to make a drastic, intentional change.

Tech time-outs are part of the cure for breaking this addiction. Not only do they help you do better work, but they can also reenergize your life in surprising ways. What will you do with the time you create? Connect with your family on a deeper level? Start a new hobby? Really commit to getting that big promotion? There's only one way to find out ...

## How to Take a Tech Time-Out

A tech time-out is a practical, and powerful, way to turn down the noise in your everyday work and life. Every professional should make a conscious decision to do this, even though it may be very difficult initially. Think of it like a time-out or halftime in a sports event, like a basketball, soccer, or football game. It's a chance to stop the clock and make adjustments.

A few tips:

**Determine your current level of tech-related dependence.** Do an informal assessment of your cumulative level of screen time. Do you reach for your phone whenever you've got some downtime? Are you constantly connected to Bluetooth? Do you feel compelled to check your email every five minutes? Do you catch yourself mindlessly scrolling through Instagram or TikTok instead of working?

You can track some of these things on your phone. For example, using iPhone's Screen Time feature and Android's Digital Wellbeing feature, you can learn how much time you spend using various apps and track how often you pick up your phone.

Where are you right now? Is your usage where you would like it to be, or is there room for improvement? Don't feel bad if your tech time is off the charts right now. I struggle with this, too. This is hard, and it is going against the grain of what's normal today. But it's totally doable.

**Recognize that you have all the power.** This is a big mind shift that will help you opt out of the madness: *you* get to say when you're connected and when you're off the grid. My phone used to be my boss. When it would ring, I would jump to attention. My email controlled my fate. When I got a new message, I would drop everything to respond. But we can all determine when and where we use our devices. It's a choice, and it is life-changing.

**Change the alerts and notifications on your smartphone.** Most people have a Pavlovian response to the telltale ping of their devices. Without thinking, we stop what we're doing to look at a screen. (And while these notifications disrupt our focus, they rarely improve our lives in any meaningful way.) Hit mute, opt out of alerts, and customize your settings so you won't be unexpectedly disturbed during critical periods of focus. If you need a quick fix to silence your cell phone, turn on airplane mode. These are simple ways to stop some of the noise.

**Put your devices somewhere else . . .** Separate yourself physically from your smartphone and digital devices during the workday. Put them in a drawer or in your bag and don't think about them at all. Put your charging station in another room or area, far enough away that you don't see them and aren't tempted to use them. You can also do this with your laptop or tablet; for example, don't bring it to a meeting or working lunch. At night, charge your phone somewhere other than your nightstand, and get an old-school alarm clock instead.

**. . . In fact, power them off altogether.** Turn off the tablet, the smartphone, the smartwatch, and the computer. Power them down and forget they're there. Experiment with tech-free times to see what's possible and what works best for you. Try it for an hour. An afternoon. All day on Sundays. All weekend long.

**Reach for paper, a pen, and a notebook instead.** You may not always need screens to do your best work. Even professionals who use screens all day can reduce their tech load at various points during the day, such as during meetings, while brainstorming alone or with a group, and (obviously) during quiet time. If possible, go low tech throughout your day and see what happens. Sit with your thoughts and something to write with. It's really all you need.

**Use the 7-to-7 rule.** What is your first thought of the day? What is your last thought? Chances are, it involves checking your smartphone for updates. My personal 7-to-7 rule will help you break this habit and become more intentional with your use of technology.

To use this rule, put your phone and other devices away beginning at 7 PM, and don't check them again until 7 AM the next day. If this time window doesn't make sense for you, choose one that does. The point is to set boundaries around screen time and provide time for more enriching activities (including quiet).

To learn more, check out the *Just Saying* podcast, episode "Tech Timeouts": podcast.thebrieflab.com/ep-209-tech-timeouts.

When in doubt, remember: you're the boss of your phone (not the other way around). Today, I manage technology that once managed me 24/7. Ironically, one "benefit" is that I often forget where my phone is—but realize if I don't have it with me, I obviously don't need it. If I can do it, so can you. Once our tech use is under our control, it will give us freedom for quiet time.

## BRIEFLY STATED

Technology won't stop until we make it stop. You don't need to constantly be tethered to technology. You'll survive without it. And you'll be surprised at how much the break will improve things for you.

## QUIET CONSIDERATIONS

**DO I**: find myself conditioned to glance at every alert and check information that does not add value to my life?

**WOULD I**: be able to set clear boundaries and commit to the 7-to-7 rule, freeing up time for quiet in ways that will benefit me and enhance my creativity, productivity, and wellness?

**CAN I**: accept that not everything is an emergency, knowing I can turn down the devices and step away from them without dire consequences?

# PART FOUR

# QUIET PLACES AND PROGRAMS

The workplace is designed almost exclusively for constant collaboration: open floor plans, constant connectivity, and a free flow of communication. A critical part of work is missing in the workday: time to actually think alone. In such a busy, noisy environment, professionals are hard-pressed to find a time and place for it during the workday. Carving out pockets of quiet time and designating places to get quiet work done actually accelerates and improves the quality of our collaboration and levels of our productivity. We need to create social norms, best practices, and boundaries together to create a culture for quiet where we have times and places to think, say, and do the most important things more often.

# Chapter 14

# Creating a Culture of Quiet

W orkplace culture has a huge impact on organizational success—or lack thereof. But sadly, many companies struggle to
build a culture that achieves its goals and satisfies its employees. This isn't that surprising, given that culture is a bit of a squishy topic.

To de-squish-ify it a bit, let's start with a simple definition: culture is
the collection of values, beliefs, and expectations that influence how people act—or don't—in a certain way. The culture sets and reinforces the
"rules," be they written or (as is typically the case) unwritten.

Some organizations have a culture of integrity, customer service, or
excellence. Others can embrace one of intensity, selflessness, or even fun.

Culture generally develops over the course of many years, becoming
firmly entrenched and, frankly, somewhat challenging to change. The
problem is that a long-established culture can work *against* an organization's stated goals.

For instance, many workplaces today consciously and unconsciously
create cultures where too much collaboration (TMC) and too much information (TMI) are the dominant workstyles. They promote an ideal of
busyness by normalizing constant meetings, interruptions, distractions,

talking on the fly, and *doing* before *thinking*. A culture steeped in TMI and TMC leaves little or no time for the thinking and planning that spurs innovation and productivity.

In other words, it leaves no time for quiet.

When organizations recognize a culture they've fallen into, it's safe to assume they'd want to change it to become more intentional. As I mentioned before, change is not an easy task. It won't happen overnight. However, if everyone understands the benefits—not just to the company but also to them, personally—it *will* happen.

Below is a construct for changing a workplace's culture. It will guide you through the steps and requirements for making the shift you desire and helping change stick. A close friend and client, John Borta, shared this with me many years ago while I collaborated with him at Grainger, a large industrial distributor.

## Three Core Beliefs About Culture

First things first, it's important to understand that there are three core beliefs about organizational culture. If you want to change a culture in any regard, get leaders and employees to agree on the following:

1. **Culture can be measured.** The impact of quiet on an organization isn't "fuzzy." It is something that can be quantified. This can be done through formal assessments, surveys, and observations of certain behaviors. At the end of the culture shift toward quiet, the organization should be able to answer questions like:

    What does the culture of a quiet organization look like? Feel like?

    How do we value concentration?

    How do we overvalue collaboration and busyness?

    How does quiet contribute to productivity?

How do we protect against distractions and disruptions?

Where and when do we find time to work alone?

How does quiet impact effectiveness and efficiency?

2. **Culture change is everyone's responsibility.** A culture change of quiet touches everybody, and likewise everybody must own the transformation. A few owners alone can't and won't make it happen. It's like a fish swimming upstream.

3. **Culture either enables or inhibits strategy and execution.** Everyone should understand how quiet relates to the overall strategy and execution of the business. Making sure everyone truly gets it vastly improves the odds that they'll embrace the needed changes. They all have a stake in making sure the company thrives.

## Five Keys to a Culture of Quiet

Here are the five truths that will help you build a culture of quiet in your organization:

1. **A culture of quiet starts with executive sponsorship.** Someone in senior leadership must embrace the vision of a quiet workplace and support and promote it. When those in the C-suite commit to new habits and behaviors, it gets others in the organization on board.

2. **It is developed by leaders who serve as teachers and practitioners.** Leaders should take ownership of practicing, fine-tuning, and demonstrating what quiet looks like to the rest of the employees. For example, a leader can open and end meetings with a few minutes of silence. Leaders can schedule buffers for quiet in between their meetings and talk about the difference they have made. They can give people autonomy to step away for time alone without fear of reprisals.

3. **It involves everyone.** A few individuals working in isolation cannot change a culture. Every person in the organization must take part in the shift to create a new social norm. This means encouraging, allowing, and trusting employees at all levels to use quiet as an ingredient in their daily work.

4. **It grows by sharing stories and evidence of successes.** Socialize and spread the word across teams and groups in the organization. Share what's working (and what is not): "Hey, we're taking morning and afternoon tech time-outs over here in HR. Why don't you folks in Marketing give it a try?" People can share stories about how quiet works, and over time the culture change will happen organically, bottom to top and top to bottom.

5. **At some point, "ownership" of quiet is transferred to the business leader.** The executive sponsor gets the ball rolling and provides ongoing support, but it's the business leader who will ensure that employees are using quiet to maximize their work. This leadership responsibility means that it is formally known to the organization and is part of how performance is measured.

### Quiet Afternoons:
### A Leadership-Sponsored Experiment

A recent *Wall Street Journal* article discussed the end-of-the-workday "dead zone" that many organizations experience. Employees are now taking flex time between the hours of 4 PM and 6 PM to pick up their children or beat the traffic and are making up that time later in the evening.[1] This behavior is a holdover from the COVID-19 pandemic, but many believe it is here to stay in the era of hybrid work. Microsoft has even dubbed this phenomenon the "Triple Peak Day," noting that knowledge workers who once had two productivity peaks in their workday now have a third peak in the hours before bedtime.[2]

What does this mean for quiet workplaces? It *could* mean the final hour or so of the workday is an excellent time for organization-wide quiet. This creative use of the end of the workday gives employees the quiet they need while making use of a time when employees are already likely to be less productive. It's a great example of a leader-led initiative to get everyone practicing quiet. If 4 to 5 or even 4:30 to 5 were to become quiet time, how might your employees and the organization benefit?

There's only one way to find out, but I predict employees would use the time to clear their minds, get their planners in order for the next day, think about their client's needs, facilitate concise communication with their teams and managers, and unlock creative ideas ready to be born. Try it out for a month and see how company-wide quiet improves your culture.

## The Quiet Revolution, A Case Study: Turning a Collaborative Culture into One That Works

It's one thing to read a list of directives on how to change your company's culture on paper. It's another thing entirely to see the process come to life in an organization. Here is a fictional case study I've written to illustrate what a Quiet Revolution might look like in action:

In the bustling realm of the software technology industry, Software BEYOND found itself ensnared in a culture that prioritized constant collaboration at the expense of individual concentration. Enter Emily Turner, a senior director and software engineer with an innovative vision. Emily's motivation to lead a transformational shift toward a quieter workplace stemmed from her deep understanding of the perils of excessive collaboration at the risk of time alone for her to work deeply on what mattered to her clients. Her tenacity and vision transformed Software BEYOND's culture and helped them overcome the risks associated with the status quo approach.

### The Constant Risks of Over-Collaboration

The Software BEYOND culture of over-collaboration had severe repercussions across various aspects of the organization. The flood of ideas and frequent changes in project direction and product development led to missed deadlines and frustrated clients. This constant churn in project direction not only risked alienating clients but also strained resources and impacted the morale of employees striving to keep up with the constant changes.

In a hybrid work environment, excessive collaboration left remote employees feeling overwhelmed and disconnected. This not only hindered their productivity but also introduced inefficiencies into the workflow. With real-time updates and impromptu meetings, remote team members struggled to keep pace, often feeling left out of crucial discussions and decision-making processes.

Clients, the lifeblood of any technology company, grew increasingly frustrated with the organization's lack of progress. Constant changes in project scope led to uncertainty and dissatisfaction, eroding trust and putting valuable client relationships at risk. The status quo approach of constant collaboration was threatening the very foundation of Software BEYOND's success.

### The Vision for Change (Get Ready for Resistance)

Emily's vision aimed to tackle these risks head-on by introducing a culture that balanced collaboration and focused work. Her journey to instigate a

"Quiet Revolution" was not without its challenges, but it ultimately proved to be the antidote to Software BEYOND's woes.

Emily faced resistance from other senior leaders and colleagues who were entrenched in the status quo. Their skepticism was palpable, and the risks of disrupting established norms were daunting. However, Emily's approach to overcoming this resistance was both strategic and persistent as she built a compelling case for change to persuade executive leadership to embrace and support her vision.

To start, she meticulously gathered evidence to demonstrate the benefits of a quieter workplace. She presented data from academic studies, industry best practices, and real-world examples, highlighting the tangible advantages of reduced noise and interruptions. Her one-on-one meetings with senior leaders were crucial in addressing their concerns directly. She tailored her arguments to align with the company's strategic goals, emphasizing how a quieter culture could give them a competitive edge, and she encouraged senior leadership to model these practices in their daily work.

Emily also introduced practical demonstrations to illustrate the benefits of a quieter culture. Quiet Zones within the office space, initially met with skepticism, provided tangible proof that focused work could lead to increased productivity. Fewer meetings that were longer and better organized also made a positive impact. Collaborative workshops allowed employees to voice their concerns, share stories of success, and contribute to the development of new workplace practices and clearer boundaries between collaborative time and quiet concentration. Additionally, Emily led her own team in implementing several simple, practical quiet work practices, showcasing the benefits of the Quiet Revolution through real-world results.

## The Transformation and Its Impact

The transformation initiated by Emily had a profound impact on her company, addressing the risks posed by the status quo approach. Product

157

development became more deliberate and focused, leading to improved alignment with client needs and fewer missed deadlines. Teams began to prioritize thorough market research, customer feedback analysis, and in-depth planning during dedicated quiet hours. This resulted in more successful product launches and increased client satisfaction.

In the hybrid work environment, the adoption of structured collaboration hours and asynchronous communication practices improved the harmony between office-based and remote employees. Remote team members felt included and less overwhelmed, fostering a more productive team dynamic. Collaboration, once hindered by real-time updates, became more thoughtful and intentional.

Trust was rebuilt with clients as the organization delivered on its promises. It retained valuable clients and deepened existing partnerships. Clients appreciated the professionalism and commitment displayed by employees, resulting in more-productive client meetings, clearer project expectations, and an improved overall client experience.

Employees themselves underwent a behavioral transformation. Company surveys reported reduced stress levels, better work–life balance, and increased job satisfaction. The reduction in constant interruptions and the introduction of focused, uninterrupted work allowed workers to regain a sense of control over their tasks. Burnout decreased, and employee retention improved as they enjoyed the benefits of a quieter and more purposeful work culture.

Innovation and creativity flourished as employees tapped into their creativity during quiet work hours. They felt empowered to share and explore new concepts, resulting in the development of novel features and solutions that garnered positive attention from clients and the industry. The quieter culture nurtured an environment where employees could think deeply, innovate freely, and contribute meaningfully to its success.

Emily's cultural transformation led to more structured and organized client interactions, resulting in a more positive client experience. The professionalism and commitment exhibited during those interactions translated into increased client satisfaction and stronger, more fruitful client relationships.

## Conclusion

Emily Turner's Quiet Revolution project was a testament to her tenacity and vision. It not only transformed the culture but also mitigated the risks associated with an overabundance of collaboration. The organization emerged as a more balanced, productive, and client-focused entity, with employees experiencing the benefits of a quieter and more purposeful work culture. Emily's journey serves as a powerful example of how innovation and determination can drive positive change even in the face of entrenched resistance. The Quiet Revolution not only reshaped Software BEYOND but also laid the groundwork for a more successful and sustainable future.

## How to Measure Success and Keep It Going

Let's assume that you—like Emily Turner—have launched a Quiet Revolution within your own organization. What needs to happen next? Ideally, following a culture shift, you will assess how far you've come. Here are the steps to measure your success.

*First, create a benchmark and survey progress.* Track your progress over time. We have created the Quiet Quiz as a team assessment to gauge progress over time in key areas like distractions and noise management. To take the quiz, visit quietworkplace.scoreapp.com. Checking in quarterly or semiannually will provide indicators of progress or issues to be addressed.

*Then, regularly share success stories.* Keep your changes alive and evolving through vignettes of progress and small victories. If a team adopts specific practices to ensure greater focus, those wins should be documented and shared with others to encourage them.

The following suggestions might help you create a sustainable culture of quiet at work:

- **Make the connection clear.** Make sure people understand your company mission, vision, and/or values and how moving to a culture of quiet will help everyone live them.
- **Paint the picture.** Also make sure they truly understand what quiet looks like and what they're allowed and expected to do. People may not *really* believe it's okay for them to sit quietly and read at work, for instance. If they suspect it's not okay, they won't do it, and nothing will change.
- **Check in with them.** Regularly hold conversations around quiet with employees. Ask them how the culture change is going. What's working for them? What isn't? What might work better? It's so important to get their input.
- **Recognize obstacles.** If someone identifies a barrier, do everything in your power to remove it.
- **Teach each other.** If something is working well for one department or even one person, ask them to share what works with others.
- **Celebrate wins.** Order in lunch for everyone or give people half a day off. Connect the win back to the benefit of infusing quiet into the culture. This keeps momentum going.

Systematically doing these things will demonstrate the shift toward a culture of quiet. Remember, it doesn't have to happen overnight. You can go at your own pace and do what is right for your organization. But when the transformation is complete and at last you are a Quiet Workplace, you will be truly amazed by how far you've come. You will see in the upcoming chapters how this shift to quiet can be successfully applied in varied scenarios and conditions.

## BRIEFLY STATED

Though an organization's culture develops over a long period of time and becomes deeply ingrained in practices and habits, a culture of quiet can emerge with clear directives from the top and participation and implementation at all levels.

## QUIET CONSIDERATIONS

**DO I:** see the need for a culture shift toward more scheduled quiet in my organization?

**WOULD I:** be able to establish a systematic plan, using the five keys to a culture of quiet, to build more opportunities for quiet throughout the day?

**CAN I:** impact the company culture by holding all stakeholders accountable for maintaining a culture of quiet?

# Chapter 15

# Quiet Works for Leaders— Going It Alone

We talked earlier in the book about why a scattered, disorganized leader who thinks on the fly is a misleading leader. If you don't consistently spend time in quiet, you run a high risk of not knowing what you want, changing direction often, confusing others, and zigzagging your way toward goals—assuming you even know what the goals are.

As you know, quiet is the solution to these problems. It's the key to understanding what really matters and clarifying the direction where you want to head. Only then can you lead others and become a true asset to your organization and employees. And having experienced the transformative power of quiet firsthand, you'll be well equipped to share it with others.

But here's the truth: you might have to go on this quiet journey alone initially. Fellow leaders might not be on board even if you enthusiastically offer your insights, and it may take time for the information to trickle down to the people you manage.

That's okay—but know that this can be lonely work. You will likely be dealing with hundreds, even thousands, of people who don't practice—or even know about—quiet (yet). But, in time, you can lead a top-down shift that changes everything.

We'll get to the steps of your journey of becoming a quiet professional shortly. But first, I want to make sure you have the time and space required to make this change stick. If you're like many busy leaders, people are competing for your attention and the extra space on your calendar is scarce. This is to be expected, but it also means you need to set some boundaries around your time. Read on to learn how.

## Are You Too Available at Work? Six Ways to Establish Healthier Boundaries

It's no secret that being a leader puts you in the position of being constantly disrupted. I got my first taste of this when I was promoted to a senior VP position at a major marketing agency in Chicago. Wanting to send the right message to my team, I made it clear that my door was always open and that I was never too busy to answer their questions. This was coming from a good place, but I went about it the wrong way, and my open-door policy came back to bite me—because every time I was deeply engaged in my own work, people would approach me.

You might feel like you can't do anything about this. After all, your job is to lead others, and this means having a certain amount of face time with those you lead. But you *can* do this part of your job while respecting your own need for quiet.

Trust me when I say this pays off for everyone involved. Quiet helps you be a better leader to your team, and you'll feel better too once you have more balance in your day.

Here are six suggestions to help you curb your availability:

**Don't always say "sure."** You might believe that a good leader always says, "Sure, I've got a minute" when approached by an employee. Resist this temptation—because those spontaneous chats can add up and steal your time. If you truly do have a moment, go ahead and have the conversation, but don't make it your default response. That feeds the illusion of immediacy under which many companies operate, and it trains people to come calling, believing you'll drop everything for them. If you make it slightly more difficult for others to access you at any time, they will be more likely to respect your time and make an appointment.

**Learn to say, "No, not now."** Remember, this is an effective strategy because the word *no* is definitive. Plus, you have the power to tell the other person when you *will* be available in the same breath: "No, I don't have time right now ... but I will in an hour." This gives you control and lets them know when to come back. And on a side note, this phrase is also a good way to manage all manners of noise. Whenever anything tempts or distracts you—anything from text messages to the chatty coworker one cubicle over—say, "No, not now."

**Ask, "How much time do you need?"** People assume that you have the time they need, but often they don't voluntarily tell you how much time that is. In fact, they likely haven't thought about how much time it is going to take at all. So ask them to think about it. If they tell you, "This conversation will take about five minutes," and you are available to talk, hold them to that time limit.

**Ask, "Did you prepare?"** Don't say it rudely, but ask, "Have you prepared what you're going to talk to me about?" All too often in office environments, or even in remote work situations, employees impulsively have a thought and then go to others for discussion. But they haven't yet thought carefully about their topic, recommendation, or request. So they talk on the fly, and it can be confusing and time consuming. Taking time to prepare is critical. If you find that someone hasn't done so, ask them to go prepare and come back when they're ready to talk clearly and concisely.

**Set a schedule for yourself.** Look at your existing schedule and see how you're organizing the day. Do you have hours blocked out when you're offline and unavailable? If not, start doing this now. In the absence of an emergency, people should know when not to contact you during the workday as well as after hours. Remember, if you don't schedule time when you should not be disturbed, you're telling others you're available to them all day.

**Find a place to "escape."** People will always know where to find you when you're sitting in your office or work area. If you want to avoid interruption, remember that you may be able to establish set times when you have the option to physically go somewhere else. Maybe it's a conference room or another unoccupied office or cubicle (there are likely plenty in our era of remote and hybrid work.) And if you're working remotely, simply turn off notifications and get offline. These are handy "escape hatches" you can utilize if you need to.

If you do these things in a thoughtful, deliberate way, you'll gain some valuable time throughout the day to explore the world of quiet. And when you *are* available to others, you're going to feel great about collaborating and conversing with them. You'll be able to be fully present in the moment and give them the gift of your undivided attention, guilt free.

> To learn more, check out the *Just Saying* podcast, episode "Feeling Obligated to Always Be Available": podcast.thebrieflab.com/ep-241-feeling-obligated-to-always-be-available.

You have created some open space in your mind and on your calendar. It's now time to get down to brass tacks and learn to become a quiet leader. Remember, it will take time to make these new habits stick. Go at your own pace, certainly, but do commit your energy to this endeavor. When you give quiet a chance, you will make strides toward becoming the leader you want to be. And of course, if you or other leaders in your organization need help, contact us at the Quiet Workplace by visiting thequietworkplace.com/programs.

## How to Become a Quiet Leader

**Start thinking of quiet as a necessity, *not* a luxury.** Many, if not most, executives need to ditch their "badge of busyness" and adopt the belief that a habit of daily quiet is necessary for success. This means that you don't just do it when you have the time—you make time no matter what. This might be a completely different way of approaching work for you, and you will need to accept that it may feel weird to make such a drastic mind shift. You will know you've embraced it when you routinely start and end your day with quiet.

Daily quiet is essential because this is when you make your game plan for whatever is coming next. Think of it this way: no coach would ever start a game by saying, "I haven't thought about this game, but let's just see what happens." But a lot of leaders dive into their workday with no preparation, and the ensuing chaos seems normal. Don't be one of them. You need a plan. Starting and ending your day with nonnegotiable quiet time is your chance to create a game plan.

To see where you are right now, ask yourself the following questions:

- Do I have a mindset of "go, go, go, noise, noise, noise"?
- Do I let my environment dictate how I think?
- Do I view quiet as a luxury or a necessity?

Your answers will let you know how you feel right now about quiet. You may be all in and ready to fundamentally change the way you work to maximize your effectiveness. That's great! Or maybe you still feel hesitation. If so, reread chapter four, "Thoughtless, Scattered Leaders Scare Us," for inspiration. The sooner you go all in, the better off you'll be.

**Use quiet to prepare for the upcoming engagements of the day.** Every executive has appointments and meetings on their calendar. But not every executive makes a habit of preparing for those engagements. Look at your planner and ask: Have I taken time to think about who I will be talking to this morning/afternoon? What are we going to talk about? What do I hope to achieve? Have I mentally prepared for this moment?

These questions are so critical for bringing your best self to each and every appointment. Without thinking about who you will be meeting and what they and you need out of the exchange, you're stepping onto the field without warming up. It's a sure way to make a subpar impression or waste everyone's time.

**Look at your calendar daily. Where is the white space?** If every appointment in your day bumps up against the next, you have a calendar management problem. But more importantly, you have a *noise management* problem. Make sure there is some white space in the morning, in the middle of the day, and in the afternoon dedicated to quiet.

On a related note, be sure that you schedule in a little breathing room before and after your meetings. It's all too easy to pack your day chock-full of appointments with no gaps between them because it makes you feel productive. There's no thoughtfulness in this approach. To use a sports metaphor, this would be like playing a game without any time-outs. You will have lost the day before you even start.

**Don't be afraid to close your door (if you have one).** If you have an office with a door, talk to the people that work with you and let them know what your closed door means. You can tell them, "When I have my door shut, it's not because I'm being rude or because I don't care about you and your needs. It's because I am trying to be more thoughtful and prepared throughout the day and need silence to do this. I am simply getting ready for what's next."

I know this flies in the face of what a lot of executives believe good leadership to be. But I believe we shouldn't have open-door policies across the board. Sometimes it's best for everyone when leaders have (momentarily) closed-door policies.

**Set examples of quiet culture.** Even if you're going on this journey alone right now, you can still set an example for those in your orbit. You might even get a few converts by showing how great a quieter office can be. Here are a few ways to introduce a culture of quiet to others:

- **Start your meetings with a few moments of quiet.** Begin meetings with two to three minutes of silence so everyone can read the agenda and write down what they're hoping to accomplish in your time together. This is a great way to share silence's effectiveness with others while getting the team aligned and focused. Amazon's Jeff Bezos does something similar. Years ago, he banned Power-Point presentations in the organization and created a new meeting structure in which every attendee silently reads a memo for the first thirty minutes of the meeting. Bezos said this was "supposed to create the context for what will then be a good discussion."[1]

- **Stop calling people when they're unavailable.** If you're consistently calling on your subordinates on the weekends and evenings without permission, that's a problem for them and for you. (It means that you don't respect their boundaries.) Stop this immediately. You can even tell people that you are making a new effort to respect their time. Then stick to your word.

- **Avoid drive-bys from above.** Have you ever felt irritation when someone knocks on your door unannounced? Well, employees feel the same way when you do this to them. And leaders frequently disrupt their subordinates, so they might be even more annoyed than you! Stop doing "drive-bys." Instead, say, "I need about five minutes of your time. Can we talk now, or should I come back later?" Better yet, get on *their* calendar for a meeting.

**Establish your ideal ratio for collaborative versus quiet time.** How much quiet do you need to perform at your best? Start by estimating your current collaborative versus quiet time ratio. Is it 10:0, or maybe 8:1? Try to lower the difference until you reach the balance you desire. The higher your leadership level, the lower your ratio should be because, of all the people in the organization, leaders should be spending the most time thinking and reflecting. Aim for somewhere in the 4:1 range rather than the 10:1 range.

**Help others become BRIEF communicators.** Others' poor communication affects your time. That meeting that took up your entire morning didn't need to be so long, but it was because the other person didn't prepare for it. Make sure to talk frequently to others about the importance of clear and concise communication. Even drawing their attention to the problem can inspire employees to put a little more thought into their work up front. You might say something like, "Hey, it would help me a lot if when you give me the weekly update, you have prepared for it. This will save us all time and frustration."

## Is More Ever Enough? Why Leaders Should Settle for *Sufficiently* Informed

There's a fallacy in leadership that "more is more." More clients, more collaboration, more communication, more explaining. I couldn't disagree *more* with this philosophy. We live and work in a world of more, but it's not giving us what we want or need. Wanting more doesn't make us content, happy, or grateful. It leaves us hungry and unsatisfied.

Speaking of hunger, I recently had lunch at a Jimmy John's restaurant where I saw a sign on the wall that echoed this very sentiment. It said, "The gap between more and enough never closes." Jimmy John is right. If we believe we can never have enough, then we will always want more. But when we put enough *before* more, the gap goes away.

This became even more evident during the COVID-19 pandemic. As people tried to learn more information about what was going on in the country and the world, they grew increasingly anxious as noise took over. That's why, in 2020, we started coaching clients to help them recognize the difference between being *sufficiently informed* and *well informed*. If we don't draw a line in the sand, we will succumb to the noise.

It's true in life and in leadership. People will overexplain if you let them. They falsely believe more is more. In truth, *less is more*. It creates torque and power. This is why I urge you to put *enough* before *more*. The gap soon goes away, and you'll find yourself saying, "I don't want more. I want enough. I want to be sufficiently informed!"

**To learn more, check out the *Just Saying* podcast, episode "When Is More Enough?": podcast.thebrieflab.com/ep-243 -when-is-more-enough.**

Any of the above tactics alone can help you maximize opportunities for quiet. When you combine them all, they can change everything about the way you work.

So far, I've shared some of the big-picture tactics for making quiet a part of your day. Here are some additional insights from a fellow leader who believes in the power of silence.

## Guest Perspective: Why Leading with Solitude Is More Important Than Ever Before

By Michael S. Erwin, author of the books *Leadership Is a Relationship: How to Put People First in the Digital World* and *Lead Yourself First: Inspiring Leadership Through Solitude* and the *Harvard Business Review* article "In a Distracted World, Solitude Is a Competitive Advantage"

Bringing your best self to work has always been a tough job for leaders. But today it's harder than ever. *Everyone* wants a piece of your time. Distractions abound. Information floods our minds, inboxes, and newsfeeds, and with the rise of AI upon us, it will only become harder to tell what is valuable and what is noise. Through it all your job is to make good decisions—for your organization, for your employees, and for yourself. If you don't get those decisions right, everyone suffers.

This is why it's up to every leader to make time to think, analyze, focus, make wise decisions, and, finally, reflect on those decisions and learn from them. This is something I talk a lot about in *Lead Yourself First* and something I have committed to doing in my own life. The only way to do this is through solitude, or quiet.

Quiet is one of the best ways to calm yourself amid stress and chaos. It enables you to work through problems and find the path forward. But practicing quiet isn't easy. It can be uncomfortable to sit with our thoughts, especially when the culture in leadership has long been focused on collaboration. Regardless, this is still the best way to be more present, show up as the leader you want to be, and get things done.

Here are some of the ways quiet benefits leaders:

**Quiet promotes effectiveness.** When you have a chance to stop and think, you become far more effective in your work and life. You make better decisions. You feel more composed. Your words carry more weight because you can say what you mean and communicate it clearly to others. (This also makes you more credible.)

**It impacts how you show up at work (and in life).** When you have no quiet time to think, analyze, focus, and reflect, it can negatively impact your life and the lives of colleagues, friends, and families. You're more likely to be agitated and stressed. Interactions might be tense. You may use a tone of voice or speak words you later regret. Clearly, this can harm relationships and make your life that much harder. But stepping away physically and psychologically for quiet brings perspective and helps negative feelings fade. Then you can return as the best version of you.

**It gives you a "longer fuse."** When you are angry or frustrated, it not only comes across to those around you, but it also wastes time. Because when you are angry and take it out on others, they get upset. Then you lose credibility and connection with people and must work to repair the relationship. Far better to use solitude to do the inner work so you can be calm and professional when it counts.

In *Lead Yourself First*, I shared a story about a former Army officer and mom of six, Dina Brager, who shared her philosophy about anger. She said that she decided she would only get mad at her kids when and if she *chose* to—if there was a purpose for the anger and if it was leading toward something productive. Once again, quiet has the power to give you the composure you need to take a breath, calm down, and choose the best way to respond.

**Quiet improves your quality of life over the long haul.** Success takes time. If you're in your career for the long game, then you'll be working hard for multiple decades, which can and often does lead to burnout. Taking breaks for solitude makes you a healthier and more balanced person and gives you the longevity you need to withstand the stressors of the daily grind and invest in your career long term.

**It helps you lean into your best human characteristics.** Spending time in quiet helps you sharpen those character strengths that make us human—enthusiasm, curiosity, kindness, braveness. In an increasingly AI-dominated world, these human skills will keep you competitive by enabling you to connect and build relationships.

**Quiet helps you stay in the present (that's where the joy is).** The busier you are, the more likely you are to keep moving and miss the joy of living in the moment. Too many people do this every day, pushing through whatever is in front of them just to get to the next thing. Your quiet time is a great way to intentionally slow down to savor what's happening right now. This makes you a better listener, deepens your relationships, and helps you get to know yourself better, too.

That's a lot of reasons to give solitude a chance. Here are some things you can start doing right now to use, infuse, and model quiet for others:

**Set expectations for your team.** Leaders set the tone for everyone, so speak often about quiet and encourage your team to make time for reflection and solitude. For example, if every time you email an employee, you get an ill-prepared response right away, ask them to take a minute or two to reflect before they hit send. If you notice that an employee has no time on their calendar to slow down, think, and prepare, challenge them to take a half hour to forty-five minutes for quiet and see what changes they notice. Remind your employees that a little quiet goes a long way.

**Stop scheduling back-to-back meetings . . .** Some professionals attend nonstop meetings and phone calls from the time they get to work until they leave. If you're one of them, you likely feel overwhelmed and out of control. Decision fatigue is real, and as the day goes on, we get less effective at making decisions because our brains can't analyze the information we are receiving. Start scheduling some extra time in between your meetings. Leave five or ten minutes of "breathing room" so you can take a moment to collect your thoughts, write down notes, give your brain a break, and recharge.

**. . . And cut meetings short where appropriate.** Look carefully at your schedule and find areas where you might be wasting time. Maybe one of your recurring meetings could be half an hour or forty-five minutes instead of a full hour. Or there might be some calls and meetings you don't need to attend. You could also consider attending the beginning of a meeting but leaving once you've given and received the crucial information.

**Use quiet before conversations in general.** There is no downside to finding a few minutes of solitude before you have any kind of communication or collaboration. Even thirty seconds of quiet can be effective. It gives you time to make a game plan. It helps you manage stress and anxiety. And it helps you keep your emotions in check so you don't do or say something you'll regret.

Remember—last of all—to always practice what you preach. A leader can talk about the importance of quiet, but if they clearly don't practice those values themselves, they'll come off as inauthentic and employees won't learn to practice their own solitude. But when leaders practice it themselves, it shows people what to value. It's changed my life, and I believe it can change yours. Give it a chance and find out what it can do for you.

Leaders, you owe it to yourselves to explore quiet and reap its benefits. But just as importantly, you owe it to those you lead. People learn how to better themselves by watching you—and will perhaps follow in your footsteps one day. Your approach to quiet could influence their own leadership journey someday. Talk about a legacy!

## BRIEFLY STATED

You can become an effective, quiet leader if you view quiet as a necessity, identify the disruptions and poor planning that dominate your time, and communicate clear expectations and boundaries to eliminate those disruptions.

## QUIET CONSIDERATIONS

**DO I:** jump on the hamster wheel every workday and go, go, go without time to pause, think, reflect, and prepare for what's next?

**WOULD I:** be able to help my team develop a quiet culture by practicing and exemplifying daily quiet practices as a necessity, not just a luxury?

**CAN I:** examine my own work habits, begin to set healthy boundaries and expectations for quiet and collaboration, and communicate those expectations to my team?

Chapter 16

# Quiet Works for Teams— A Bottom-Up Approach

We just talked about a top-down approach to creating a quiet workplace. But change doesn't have to *only* come from executives. In this chapter, we'll look at several bottom-up strategies for cultivating quiet. Any group of like-minded individuals can start a Quiet Revolution—and often, these grassroots efforts are more likely to take root and spread.

The great thing about creating an uprising from below is that small groups can work out the kinks before scaling and spreading their initiative throughout their team, department, or company. Who better to recognize, understand, and address employees' needs and concerns than their colleagues? (Compare this to when an organization's leadership widely disseminates a program that might be flawed or still needs work. As you can imagine, it's a night-and-day difference!)

Plus, when frontline employees are the ones to drive change, more widespread buy-in and engagement will follow. When people see a new habit being pioneered, modeled, and encouraged by their coworkers, they are more likely to enthusiastically adopt it themselves.

Every company is unique. Each has different cultures, ways of working, needs, and values. It would be impossible to create a one-size-fits-all Quiet Revolution protocol. That said, the best practices I share below will help any company make the shift toward quiet.

## Create a Quieter Company Culture, One Week at a Time

Whether or not your leadership is also exploring quiet, teams can adopt these practices to change the culture in a positive way.

If you want to create a quiet company from the bottom up, your first step should be selecting a small team—I suggest four to six people—to be "quiet ambassadors." These will be the thought leaders who really embrace change and lead by example (versus trying to get the whole organization to change at one time). Smaller teams can experiment and learn what will work and what will not in your organization.

I recommend that this initial group of quiet ambassadors meet at least once a week to discuss goals, strategies, and lessons learned. It may also be helpful to create weekly objectives or areas of focus that will build upon each other each week and serve the triple function of (1) enabling you to stay on track, (2) helping you develop your "quiet muscles," and (3) spreading the "gospel of quiet" to more people in the organization.

*To ensure that quiet ambassadors share fundamental knowledge, start a "quiet book club." My previous books, BRIEF and NOISE, build a firm foundation for the Quiet Works approach to the professional workday. I recommend starting there first, discussing insights during your weekly meetings. Then, when you're all on the same page, dig into Quiet Works and talk about it as a group. Figure out what works and what doesn't.*

While you and your fellow quiet ambassadors can and should identify weekly objectives that work for your team and organization, here is a
suggested plan for the first seven weeks. You may decide that only the core
group of quiet ambassadors will initially participate, or you might decide
to invite additional colleagues to join you as time goes by—especially if
they express curiosity or interest.

**Week One: Start with five minutes of morning quiet time.** Set aside five—
only five!—minutes at the beginning of your workday. If you can't do that,
try just one minute. The important thing is to start *somewhere*. You might
find it helpful to use an egg timer to give yourself a visual of how much time
has passed and how much time remains. (*Don't* use a timer on your phone,
though—the possibility for tech temptation or distraction is too great.)

As the days pass, consider expanding your time alone throughout the
workday to get more comfortable with the practice. Take just one minute
of quiet before you send an email, before you make a phone call, or before
you begin a difficult task.

Talk about your progress at the next team meeting. Where are you
struggling? Where are you successful?

**Week Two: Take a tech time-out.** Most people initially feel that their
productivity and creativity would take a serious hit without the help of
technology. This week is a chance to challenge yourself and learn what's
possible. To be clear, I don't expect you to completely abstain from using
technology. For better or worse, going fully analog isn't possible in many
workplaces. But there are ways to lean less heavily on devices and more
deeply into quiet.

A few suggestions:

- Attend meetings without your computer.
- Refrain from checking your emails so often; establish designated
  times to be offline.

- If you don't need it for a work-related task, put your smartphone in a desk drawer. Out of sight, *slightly* more out of mind.
- Use the 7-to-7 rule after work hours. Put your phone away for twelve hours of the day every day.
- Practice commuting to work in silence.

**Week Three: Increase your quiet time.** In addition to taking five minutes for quiet in the morning, add five minutes of quiet to your afternoon routine. This is a simple way to build on the habit—and even five minutes is enough time to create the mental space your mind craves. Between your morning quiet, tech time-outs throughout the day, and afternoon quiet, you should start to notice a shift.

**Week Four: Create Do Not Disturb spaces throughout the office.** Work as a group to select and designate some public spaces as quiet zones. You might use a spare office, a lounge area, or an entryway to your building. (Get creative!) Use signage, emails, and conversations to explain to others what the quiet zones are, how to use them (for instance, are smartphones discouraged?), and how you hope they will positively impact the organization.

**Week Five: Define when it is justified to interrupt another person's alone time.** Quiet time shouldn't be interrupted for "Hey, have you seen my stapler?" You can wait a few minutes before asking, "Would you mind resending that email?" However, an interruption may be warranted for "The CEO is on the line for you" ... and it's *definitely* necessary for "The building is on fire!"

My point is, in the event that an emergency does occur (whether it's work or disaster related), you want to have a plan. Figure out what events would warrant immediate action. Create the criteria that would justify employees being interrupted during their quiet time. Getting clear on this removes ambiguity or confusion and keeps everyone on the same page.

Likewise, hold some conversations to define less urgent events. When everyone agrees on what is critical and what can wait, it creates the potential for people to break away more frequently for uninterrupted quiet and focus. Use the Covey and/or Eisenhower Matrix discussed in chapter eleven to help you identify where scenarios might fall across the spectrums of urgent and important.

**Week Six: Create reasonable response-time windows (ranging from "nonurgent" to "hair on fire").** Once you've figured out what justifies a disruption, set some rules for managing people's expectations around communication response times. Why? Knowing that you aren't expected to immediately respond to an email or Slack message, for instance, allows you to better focus on being quiet. You won't have that little voice in the back of your mind saying, *But what if someone expects me to get back to them in the next five minutes?* (Quiet time aside, you'll be better able to manage your time and tasks, period.)

*Talking about response time and establishing expectations, rules, and workplace norms is key to a healthy organization. People become frustrated and often give up when their expectations go unfulfilled. When the boss expects an immediate response to an email but a subordinate assumes the matter can wait (and vice versa!), everyone ends up disappointed or upset. And without open discussion, it will keep happening. Chances are, right now there are no established rules—and that means anything goes.*

So, for example, if one employee sends another employee an email for a nonurgent matter, there should be a mutually agreed-upon expectation that the recipient does not need to drop everything and respond. Maybe nonurgent communications can go unanswered for half a day or even a full day. The beauty is, you get to decide what makes sense for your organization's circumstances.

On the other end of the urgency spectrum, let's say you've got an angry customer. That's likely an emergency, which means an immediate response is required (it's the equivalent of needing to wake the commander, as discussed in chapter eleven).

And then there are circumstances where response time should fall between "take your time" and "emergency." If you experience a major financial snafu or if an employee decides to quit, maybe that's a fifteen-minute response time frame. The situation is urgent, certainly, but not critical.

*You might be wondering, But how do I know for sure how urgent someone else thinks a situation is? A good strategy to minimize confusion is to make the medium the message. For example:*

- *Sending an email means it's okay to wait a day to answer.*
- *Sending a Slack message means that you should respond within a two-hour window.*
- *A text or phone call means the situation is hot—answer immediately.*

**Week Seven: Create a plan to help you stay the course.** Cultivating a quieter workplace culture won't happen in just six weeks. It is an ongoing process. Now that you've laid the foundation, it's time to think about how you would like to spread and scale quiet throughout your organization. Write a statement as a group using SMART goals to solidify your intentions. Your plan should be:

Specific: What, exactly, do you want to accomplish?

Measurable: How will you know when you've achieved your goals?

Actionable: What actions will you take to make progress?

Relevant: How will having a Quiet Workplace help you better fulfill your organization's mission and improve the culture?

Time bound: Choose a deadline (that makes sense for your organization) for achieving your goals.

———

Any group of employees, no matter how small or what their position might be on the organization's hierarchy, has the power to bring quiet into the workplace. At the very least, you'll be able to carve out a space for peace, reflection, and mutual respect within your team or department. But as your efforts become more established, don't be surprised if other colleagues take note and want to join the Quiet Revolution, too. Have as many conversations as possible about the power of quiet. In time, quiet will resonate loudly throughout more—or all—of your organization. (A contradiction? Maybe. But I'll take it!)

## BRIEFLY STATED

Leaders aren't the only ones who need quiet to be more effective. United, purposeful, driven teams can help change a company's culture of noise to a culture of quiet.

## QUIET CONSIDERATIONS

**DO I:** feel the pressure to respond to others' communications and, therefore, expect immediate responses to all of my texts, emails, and Slack messages, regardless of urgency?

**WOULD I:** benefit from examining my own communication expectations and adjusting them to a more realistic response time?

**CAN I:** eliminate noise for others by working with my team to create and adopt a methodical approach for incorporating quiet practices from the bottom up?

## Chapter 17

# Quiet Works for Coaching— The Missing Puzzle Piece for Breakthroughs

C areer and business coaching is a massive industry. According to the International Coaching Federation, there are currently 36,680 certified coaches in 134 countries.[1] In 2019, the estimated global revenue from coaching was 2.849 billion USD.[2]

More and more professionals are working with coaches to build skills and knowledge and advance their careers. Whether it's an executive, personal, performance, or life coach, it's far too easy for both parties— coaches and their clients—to skim the surface instead of going deeper to solve problems and change people's lives. No one wants to waste their time or not get their money's worth, but unfortunately it happens a lot, and both sides are usually left feeling frustrated.

Quiet can change all that. It accelerates the work you do by benefiting coaches and coaching clients alike. Quiet is the missing puzzle piece that helps everyone thrive.

I remember one of the first coaches I worked with. He was a great listener, but soon it became evident that he wasn't taking notes during our sessions together. In fact, he would ask the same questions week after week. Every meeting felt like the movie *Groundhog Day*. I would constantly have to repeat myself, re-creating the context for quiet in a noisy world.

It was then that I started thinking about creating a program through which coaches could become Quiet Works certified. I realized all coaches could serve their clients better if they utilized quiet to prepare for their meetings and reflect on the work done once they were over. I suspected this would give them time and space to think deeply about their clients' needs and help them achieve their personal and professional goals. Turns out it was a powerful accelerator for growth and progress. Today, our Quiet Works certified coaches and coaching team utilize quiet to work more effectively and efficiently with professionals, to everyone's benefit.

## Quiet Benefits Coaches

If you're a coach reading this book, the need for quiet likely resonates with you. Coaches must carefully consider their clients' needs and issues to help them reach their potential. But quality coaches don't coach by telling clients what to do. Rather, they ask powerful and reflective questions that enable the client to discover their problem areas, break through them, and get past them. The problem is, many coaches fail to spend adequate time prior to and following their calls to think and reflect on their clients' areas that need improvement. *What are my client's issues and challenges? What is the real topic they want to discuss? What is important to them? What are their blind spots?* By using quiet principles to ask these questions, coaches are better able to help clients help themselves.

Even if you believe you're already a quiet professional, you might benefit from this training. I remember a particular cohort of coaches I once worked with. At the beginning of the program, they were given the Quiet Quiz (see chapter twelve) to help them learn how much noise was impacting their environment. The individuals initially gave themselves high scores, believing they were already thoughtful, intentional practitioners. But upon retaking the test at the end of the program, their scores went down significantly. What the coaches learned surprised them: they hadn't mastered quiet . . . *yet*. But they would in the coming days, weeks, and months. And that would change everything.

Before we go any further, let's review some more insights about the art of coaching. Whether you're a coach reading this book or a professional who has sought coaching (or may do so in the future), you can keep this wisdom in mind through all stages of your career.

### A *Quiet Works* Coach's Perspective

**Don't dive into professional issues right away. Meet them where they are.** Coaches can help clients make monumental strides toward professional goals by always embodying a coaching mindset. But the *first* job of a coach is to meet the client where they are in the moment. Then cocreate your session together to cultivate trust, safety, and expectations.

**Let the client choose the topic and agenda.** Remember, it's the client's topic and agenda. Coaching isn't problem-solving. Fight the impulse to tell them what to do. Your focus should always be on your client and their story—not on your own biases and solutions.

**Believe in your client.** To serve your client, you must believe they are whole, resourceful, and creative. They are fully capable of figuring out their problems. They need a partner on their coaching journey—not a fixer.

**Focus on the client, not on the topic.** If both parties are focused solely on the topic, then you are both problem-solving. (And remember, problem-solving isn't your job.) Instead, be interested in the client's relationship *to* the topic. This is the jumping-off point that allows you to go deeper. To lead others, professionals must be able to lead themselves first—and that means digging deep to align the body, mind, and soul.

**Be agile always.** Clients may jump from one topic to the next or make leaps that others may not always follow. But a good coach can keep up and stay with their clients by being deeply present, as well as curious and empathetic. This level of agility helps you pick up on the nuances of a conversation and also ask the powerful and reflective questions at the right time. A well-timed "What are you noticing right now?" or "Where do you feel that self-limiting belief is coming from?" can help lead to big breakthroughs.

**Be quiet to be aware.** The goal in coaching is always to create greater awareness, alignment, and client growth—a balance between what it is that the client values and where they want to go. Are they living in sync with those values? Are they taking care of themselves? Are they nurturing their most important relationship? Are they making each day count? Work on these questions before leaping to professional goals. When both parties embrace quiet, it takes coaching from a transactional interaction to a transformational experience.

**Understand that without quiet, *none* of this work is possible.** The strategies above help you build the container to be a great coach. But the real secret ingredient of stellar coaching is utilizing the power of quiet. A coach's greatest superpower is listening. If you can listen carefully to your client, you'll harness a creativity that can't be matched—and you and your client together can make big things happen. But being able to listen and adapt instantaneously to what your client is saying depends on silence. Silence is the touchstone.

**The bottom line: take the time to be quiet.** It pays off for everyone. A coaching relationship is most beneficial and effective when coaches take time to reflect on their client. Only with introspection can you help them move the needle and make strides toward their goals. And introspection requires quiet.

Don't schedule your appointments back-to-back with no breathing room in between. Rather, intentionally set aside time between appointments devoted to quiet. Take five, or ten, or fifteen minutes for "clearing" so you can be present and take a step back and think deeply about your client and their needs. Reflect on how you can best serve them and take note of insights you would like to bring to the next meeting. Over time, your quiet practice will deepen your relationships, build trust, and help you help others more than you ever imagined.

## Quiet Benefits Coaching Clients, Too

Unfortunately, clients struggle with some of the same problems as do the coaches they hire. They are busy and overbooked. They often come to their coaching sessions unprepared for the meeting. They arrive late and harried, having just come from a previous call with no time to think about their goals. Instead of having a question or topic prepared, they speak off the cuff and waste most of the meeting circling around the root issue until it finally emerges. (And by the time they focus in on it, time is nearly up.) Rinse and repeat.

This isn't an efficient mode of professional growth. It slows the coaching process and frustrates both parties along the way. Further, coaching is pricey. It can cost up to $500 an hour. If clients aren't utilizing quiet to prepare for their conversations, they don't get the ROI they are paying for and deserve. Make sure you're not wasting your time or missing out.

The Quiet Works for Coaching™* program solves issues for coaches and clients by infusing quiet methodology into both sides of the relationship. This International Coaching Federation accredited program helps coaches become more effective and clients to develop faster.

But back to those of you who currently or may someday seek professional development coaching. Spending time in quiet reflection will supercharge your results. The Quiet Worksheet, below, is a tool to help you get more out of your sessions.

---

* Our program is approved and accredited by the International Coaching Federation for Continuing Coach Education (CCE) units. Quiet Works Certified Coaches earn a total of twenty CCE hours. These CCE units are awarded in two categories: (1) Core Competencies and (2) Resource Development.

## The Quiet Worksheet: A Tool for Thinking and Planning in Advance

As mentioned, the ideal way to prepare for a coaching session is by spending time thinking about the areas where you need professional development. Maybe you need to gain clarity around your career goals or learn to request and receive constructive feedback. You might need to work on leading with empathy or build a new skill. Whatever your need, it's critical to find the area of focus you want to talk about and to come prepared.

This "mind map" will help you do your thinking ahead of your coaching appointments. It was developed by two senior leaders in our organization and certified Quiet Works coaches. You can download it by visiting thequietworkplace.com/the-quiet-worksheet.

First, and prior to your meeting, identify the central issue you hope to discuss. Spend time in quiet thinking about your topic. Remember, this is your topic and your agenda.

Then use the WORKS branches to dig and explore further:

**W**: **WHY** is this topic important?
**O**: What is the **OUTCOME** you want from this conversation?
**R**: Is there a way to **REFRAME** the problem or challenge? Can you use a metaphor or analogy?
**K**: What are the **KEY DETAILS** that the coach needs to know?
**S**: Who will **SUPPORT** you? Who will hold you accountable?

Arriving prepared and ready to do the (often difficult) work of self-exploration makes the coaching journey all the more rewarding. If you want to get the most of your sessions—regardless of whether you're coaching or being coached—you've got to put in the time . . . the *quiet* time. Slow down just a little, and you'll emerge better, stronger, and faster than ever.

# QUIET WORKSHEET™

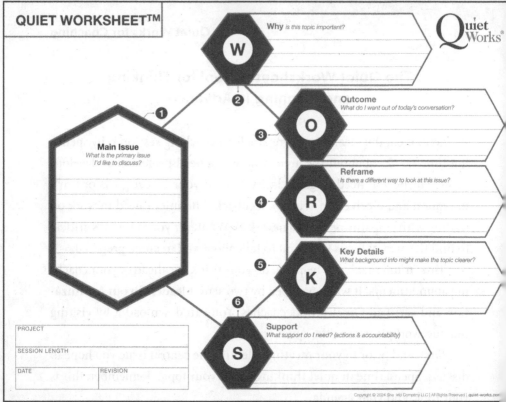

**W** — **Why** *is this topic important?*

**Main Issue**
*What is the primary issue I'd like to discuss?*

**O** — **Outcome**
*What do I want out of today's conversation?*

**R** — **Reframe**
*Is there a different way to look at this issue?*

**K** — **Key Details**
*What background info might make the topic clearer?*

**S** — **Support**
*What support do I need? (actions & accountability)*

PROJECT

SESSION LENGTH

DATE          REVISION

---

## QUIET FLOW

## NOTES TO HELP PREPARE YOUR TOPIC

### W | WHY
*"Why is this topic important to me?"*

### O | OUTCOME
*"What's the one thing I hope to take away from today's conversation?" (i.e., direction, clarity, a plan of action...)*

### R | REFRAME
*"What's my perspective of this topic?"*
*"What's the impact to me and/or others?"*
*"What's a way to describe how I'm feeling?" (i.e., metaphor, analogy, etc.)*

### K | KEY DETAILS
*"What key pieces of information do I need to share to make myself clearer?"*
*"What does my audience need to know?"*
*"What background info would be helpful?"*

### S | SUPPORT
*"What support do I need from you/others?"*
*"What action(s), next steps will I take before the next conversation?"*
*"Who is my accountability partner?"*

### HELPFUL TIPS

- TAKE SEVERAL MIN OF QUIET TO THINK ABOUT THE TOPIC
- BE INTENTIONAL - FILL OUT BOXES #1, #2, #3
- USE THE REST OF YOUR TIME FOR #4 AND #5
- BOX #6 - IS YOUR ACTIONS, FILLED OUT AT THE END OF THE COACHING SESSION
- NEXT SESSION, CHECK IN ON #6 AND CONTINUE OR MOVE TO ANOTHER TOPIC (REMEMBER IT'S YOUR AGENDA)

To learn more about the Quiet Works for Coaches program, please visit thequietworkplace.com/programs/quiet-works-for -coaches.

## BRIEFLY STATED

Since more and more professionals are seeking out life, business, and executive coaches to improve their performance, planning, and management skills, coaches must learn to tune in and truly listen to their clients in order to successfully work together. Quiet is the key.

## QUIET CONSIDERATIONS

**DO I:** have opportunities to work with coaches who encourage me to improve through preparation, reflection, exploration, and listening?

**WOULD I:** benefit from working with a coach to develop more leadership skills and strategies to adapt to a wide variety of business applications?

**CAN I:** utilize the Quiet Worksheet to help in defining central issues and in planning for coaching sessions—either as a coach myself or as a client?

# Chapter 18

# Semi-Silent Summits: Why Quiet Works for Off-Sites

O ff-site meetings are often a great way for teams of professionals to step away and get meaningful work done. Off-sites drive engagement, allow people to learn new skills or plan for the future, and help remote or hybrid employees get to know each other and collaborate.

I've been to many off-site meetings in my career, and I've noticed that they almost always suffer from one fatal flaw: they are all talk and no quiet. The organizers mistake time spent together, connection, and a fun break from the norm for getting things done.

A senior military leader in Special Operations once told me a story that mirrored my observations. He had recently attended a conference with some of his fellow leaders for a two-day off-site. The agenda was packed so tightly that the attendees had no time to reflect on what the group was learning. Without time to read, think, or prepare between meetings, they only stopped at night when it was time to sleep.

This is just what we do during off-sites. We go into them for all the right reasons—ready to plan a big project, or do some team building, or shake off the cobwebs and find new creative ways to innovate. But our execution is flawed. We don't take time to design an agenda that includes time for quiet and reflection. And so our time together is wasted because there is no consideration of how the time is spent or what our intent really is.

## Current Off-Site Meeting Designs Aren't Cutting It

Here are some of the more common mistakes when groups venture off toward an off-site meeting, only to return no better off:

- Unstructured, overambitious agendas
- Dominant voices that overwhelm, with no rules of engagement
- Unclear, unpublished, and hidden agendas
- Constant, free-flowing information
- Off-track, sidebar conversations
- No time alone to process, prepare, or reflect

Semi-silent summits can change everything. This is not the same thing as a "silent retreat" that people may attend for wellness or spiritual purposes. It's still a working off-site, but it has moments strategically built in for quiet.

This makes all the difference.

This approach is impactful. Our team had our first semi-silent off-site just prior to the onset of COVID-19, in which we workshopped and re-learned the BRIEF methodology. As it turned out, this powerful getaway was the glue that held our small, remote company together through the pandemic.

Here are the requirements for a semi-silent off-site:

**A facilitator who believes in a quiet approach.** You will need a person to thoughtfully design and lead the event. Usually, people are thrust into this role, but rarely have they been trained for it. A skilled facilitator understands how to moderate, when to take a break, when an attendee is going down a rabbit hole and when to redirect them, how to prevent one dominant voice from taking over, and how to set up a room for a great group dynamic.

**A quiet-friendly location.** Different locations will suit different teams or organizations. A hotel or conference center might be right for some. A remote cabin in the woods, a campground with hiking trails, or a bed-and-breakfast might work for others. It simply must have an adequate meeting space, as well as places for small groups to break away to talk, and of course somewhere to go for silence.

**A "converge–diverge" agenda.** Thoughtfully design an agenda that allows plenty of opportunities for the group to *converge* and *diverge*. Bring people together to learn and collaborate; send them away to let them think alone. This is when they can process information, read, take notes, and develop questions, comments, and discussion points.

During our semi-silent off-site, our team benefited from quality time together and quiet time alone. We had short classes to teach our staff the communication principles we teach at The BRIEF Lab. We had mealtime together and gatherings after them to share personal stories and fun facts about each other. And we scheduled short talks from senior leaders on topics relating to our core values.

But we also had time alone. Between class sessions, there were quiet breaks to read and reflect; in the morning there was quiet time before breakfast to prepare for the day; in the afternoon we gave everyone personal, no-talk time before dinner. The structure had a nice flow to it where we knew when it was time to interact and when it was time to be alone. Most importantly, it worked to bring us together to learn communication principles and more about each other—those were the core objectives.

I can't stress enough the importance of the "diverge" portions of off-sites. When attendees are talking, listening to lectures, and collaborating, the learning happens in real time. But you simply can't fully process all the information in this manner. Small pockets of time in silence are essential for full absorption and the insights that will follow! The ratio of converge to diverge is not 1:1. You might spend fifty minutes in collaboration and need only ten minutes of quiet for incredible results.

Remember: "diverge" is not the same as a break. (Though you will need to schedule breaks as well). It is time dedicated for quiet. You might even assign a quiet task. For example: "Take ten minutes to write down the three biggest issues you're thinking about right now." Or: "Reflect on how you feel about the current state of this initiative." Or: "Take fifteen minutes in quiet to read an article that we will come back to discuss."

Further, you will need a big-picture view, as well as smaller snapshots of what the day(s) will look like:

- **Macro agenda:** What are you going to do/learn/accomplish over the course of the off-site?

and

- **Micro agenda:** What will you do during each portion of the macro agenda? (How will you start? What will be covered? How much time will be spent on each topic?)

**Time for attendees to prepare *in advance*.** Employees should have opportunities to prepare for the off-site prior to attending.

- Give them the agenda in advance, along with the objectives of the meeting. They should never see the agenda for the first time upon walking in the door at the off-site.
- Assign appropriate prework: things to read, think about, and consider.

These elements will put them in the right mindset.

**Plenty of chances to break away for quiet.** Most breakthroughs happen when people are alone, so give them ample opportunities to leave the group for solitude and reflection:

- Reading time
- Morning quiet time
- Time to take a walk
- Five minutes at the end of team time to capture discussion points
- Time to work on a specific task, prompt, or challenge
- Unstructured time for them to choose what to do

**A *minimum* definition of success.** Most groups go into an off-site with big goals. But it's more important to establish the minimum definition of success. The temptation in many meetings is to be overly ambitious and cram everything into an already tight agenda. It's unrealistic. What's more effective is to lower the bar, define what is minimally acceptable, and then try to surpass it. Setting—and exceeding—achievable goals happens when you set a minimum definition of success.

**Flexibility to bend (but not break) the agenda.** Don't be so rigid in your schedule that you ignore the needs of the group. Go into your day(s) willing to flex the schedule a bit. Be wary of pushing people past what they can do. If you sense that the group needs time away, give a break—even if it's not on the agenda.

**Social time.** Try to have time that is unstructured together so people can get to know each other, talk, and enjoy the process. A seasoned facilitator can design some fun activities for groups to not feel like it's always business.

> To learn more, check out the *Just Saying* podcast, episode "Quiet Works for Offsite Meetings": podcast.thebrieflab.com /ep-298-quiet-works-for-offsite-meetings.

What makes this type of off-site special, memorable, and (most importantly) effective is that quiet feeds conversations, collaboration, and interaction. People crave time to process and prepare—and quiet slows it all down. It's amazing how our sense of time changes when we insert silence as a small and strategic ingredient. Suddenly we can savor the entire experience.

When my company decided to open the first Quiet Workplace in Southern Pines, North Carolina, I was excited to have that location serve as a destination for quiet off-sites. We already had ample space at The BRIEF Lab next door for organized collaboration, so it only made sense to make this experience possible and re-create this space as a dedicated location that was designed for both quiet and collaboration. I will describe the Quiet Workplace in more detail in chapter twenty, but in the meantime, you can get some inspiration by taking a short tour on our website: thequietworkplace.com/programs/offsites.

## BRIEFLY STATED

Off-site meetings can be extremely beneficial for teams looking to connect and collaborate. A thoughtfully designed event centered around a quiet approach, a supportive location, and a planned agenda is the key to success.

## QUIET CONSIDERATIONS

**DO I:** plan meetings or retreats with little thought to a purposefully planned agenda with built-in opportunities for quiet reflection?

**WOULD I:** benefit from using strategies from the Quiet Workplace to help me in future planning *or* consider meeting in Southern Pines with my team to experience a Quiet Workplace in person?

**CAN I:** commit to incorporating well-designed moments for my team to converge and diverge in future meetings or off-sites?

# Chapter 19

# Quiet Works for BRIEF Communicators

A re you a BRIEF communicator? How well is it working for you?
If you're one of the thousands who have taken a previous course with The BRIEF Lab, you've already learned the skills that make you an elite communicator in a world of noise and distractions. If you're new to BRIEF communication, know that the methods we teach help you make a bigger impact, connect with people on a deeper level, and hold their attention where others can't.

It's not about charisma or personality. It's a skill set anyone can learn. And it works. I encourage those of you who haven't taken courses with us to see what The BRIEF Lab offers. Check out thebrieflab.com for more information.

But BRIEF communication only works when we *do the work*. That's where a lot of people get tripped up and end up unprepared. Many of the BRIEF trained professionals we've heard from are still not performing at 100 percent. Does this sound like you? Maybe your emails were once brief and to the point, but lately they've gotten too wordy. Or your once productive meetings with your boss are missing the mark. Maybe conversations with clients have started falling a little flat.

Would you like to take a guess at what's missing? It's time and quiet to prepare before you communicate.

## The Perils of Communicating on the Fly

In a nutshell, when we are unprepared, we speak off the cuff and our communication suffers. Nearly everyone does this, so don't feel too bad. (This is the reason I'm writing this book, to help you get in the habit of quiet preparation.) But before we get into the how-tos of improving your communication through silence, let's explore what talking, writing, and doing on the fly could be costing you.

Below I've offered a series of scenarios for your consideration. While fictional, these stories are amalgams of real-life situations I have witnessed in others or experienced firsthand. Think of them as case studies or cautionary tales. And don't forget to look for not-so-good behaviors you yourself can relate to.

### Scenario 1: It's Not Her First Rodeo ...

*A VP of sales is at a big annual conference with her team. They've got a trade show, a booth, and a packed schedule of meetings and events. The convention center is bustling with activity, and everyone on the team jumps into the fray.*

*During the next few days, this VP will have many responsibilities over the course of the conference. She'll be talking with exhibitors, prospective clients, her team, other attendees. She'll be using her phone to check emails and communicate throughout the day.*

*But the thing is, she knew this was coming—it's not her first rodeo. She knew the conference would be full of opportunities to communicate with a range of other professionals. How much time does she spend alone in silence thinking about those key conversations? How much time does she commit to reviewing her agenda? Not nearly enough.*

*Why not? Because, leading up to the beginning of the conference, she wears her busyness like a badge and lets all the things going on in life and at work justify that she will communicate in most of the interactions at this event on the fly.*

**What's the risk?** The biggest problem (among many) is that her team is not on the same page. This VP has not defined what would make a successful conference. Conversations with her team, her clients, and her prospects will be unclear, scattered, and potentially misleading.

### Scenario 2: Back to Work After a Holiday Break

*It's Monday morning and everyone is just returning to the office after a much-needed holiday break. A middle manager knows he will be seeing his coworkers, his boss, and his senior leaders for the first time in a while and that there will be opportunities to interact, engage, and catch up with them. They'll all be asking the same question: "How was your break?"*

*And like clockwork, he will respond with an uninteresting, forgettable response. Something like "Oh, it was great." How original!*

**What's the risk?** This is a missed opportunity for our manager. Post-break conversations are a great time to make real, human connections with colleagues and get to know more about their lives. These details are important threads in the fabric of real, meaningful relationships—the kind people crave. Yes, everybody says the same thing—filler words—when they come back from a holiday. But remember, our manager knows this is coming. With a little forethought, he might have answered, "It was tiring, but so fulfilling," and then asked others, "What did you do on your break? Where did you go? What was most memorable?" Without taking time to prepare, this potentially valuable moment will pass and be gone forever.

### Scenario 3: A Big Deadline Is Looming

*A team lead is working on a big project with a deadline that is coming up fast. Everyone is busy and stressed, and the pressure is mounting to get everything done. He's got the distinct feeling that time is running out. There are so many conversations to be had and so much information to share back and forth. Even though his hair is already on fire, our professional can't afford to stop or even slow down.*

*It's not as if he didn't know that all this had to get done—that there were lots of moving parts to keep in motion, plenty of people to keep updated, and milestones to reach. He's stressed, irritable, scattered, and unfocused as he puts his head down to keep working.*

**What's the risk?** This professional is neither calm nor focused. He can't do his best work because he left no time to prepare or think. So all of his interactions suffer, his teammates might not get the information they need, and they risk dissatisfying the client.

> **For more information, check out the *Just Saying* podcast, episode "Communicating on the Fly—Crash or Soar?": podcast .thebrieflab.com/ep-297-communicating-on-the-fly-crash-or -soar.**

---

Maybe in the past you've defended communicating on the fly because it seems acceptable when you're busy. Or maybe you don't believe you have the autonomy to control your own calendar. But these examples show you that the risk of crashing is very real and often imminent!

What if you wanted to soar instead?

The information in this book is meant to commence where your previous training left off and deepen your ability to communicate better. If you are a veteran of our BRIEF Lab courses, you won't want to miss our new program designed specifically for you.

## Quiet Works for BRIEF Teams

The best way to drive adoption of BRIEF communication following a course at The BRIEF Lab is a new course called Quiet Works for BRIEF Teams. You already know the methodology that can change your career and life. You've learned valuable skills such as Headlining, Trimming, and using the BRIEF Map. But if you and your teammates have struggled to put it all into action, we are here to help.

Becoming an intentional communicator doesn't happen by accident. It takes time and it takes quiet to be able to think and communicate effectively. But this is the very place where people struggle. Without the discipline to get time alone on your calendar and stick with it for the long haul, the methodology can't work.

That's where we come in.

In this four- to six-week program, your team will be broken into small cohorts, and each will be assigned a coach from the Quiet Workplace. Each week the team will come together for forty-five minutes to discuss the previous week's topics and challenges and will look ahead to the topics and challenges for the next week. They will share their challenges and their successes, and everyone will learn from each other. At the end of the course, leaders will make specific recommendations that they, their teams, and their organization need to follow as BRIEF and Quiet Works practitioners.

There are several benefits of the program:

- You have a challenge each week that is doable while still stretching you.
- You get small-group accountability, and your peers will help keep you honest.
- Your team is focused on a bigger goal as everyone becomes elite communicators and the culture begins to change.

The team aspect can't be underestimated. You've taken The BRIEF Lab courses as a team and worked with those people before. Now you're ready to take things to the next level with quiet. But if you're the only one doing it, the organizational culture won't change. When everyone takes the time to prepare their communications in advance, quiet is the rocket fuel that propels lasting change.

For more information, please visit thequietworkplace.com/programs/quiet-for-brief.

## A BRIEF Lab Coach's Perspective: Part I

### Don't Just Tour the Gym, *Get in Shape!*

A coworker said something once that really resonated with me. We had just wrapped up a training session at The BRIEF Lab when he said to me, "I feel like the team we just worked with only got to tour the gym." I asked him what he meant, and he explained that when people first visit a gym, they learn how all the machines work, but they're not in shape yet.

It makes sense. You can know the methodology for elite communication inside out, but without putting it into practice using quiet, you're not going to get clearer, more concise, or better. But when your team goes through the Quiet Works for BRIEF Teams program, they have a full workout regimen for four to six weeks to give them forward momentum. They have access to a personal trainer who will guide them along the way. They have experience working the "quiet muscles," plus a community to keep them coming to their quiet practice again and again.

You've toured the gym. Don't stop now. Keep going, and you'll be glad you did when people know you by your consistent, clear, and concise communication.

## Making Quiet Work for BRIEF Communicators

For those of you who want to get started using quiet to improve your communication right away, here are some things you can do right now. You've no doubt got colleagues and leaders who went through a BRIEF Lab course or two working by your side. Why not get them to join the effort? It will make their lives easier, too!

A few tips for forming your own BRIEF team:

**Don't go it alone!** Seek out your teammates who also took The BRIEF Lab coursework and go on the journey together. For one thing, it takes everyone pulling together to change the culture of your organization. For another, you'll benefit from the support of a group as you share your wins and struggles. You'll also learn a lot from one another.

**Build a team.** Put together a cohort of colleagues who want to practice the BRIEF methodology with you, and then choose a leader. This will keep you all accountable. Think of this group like a book club (a BRIEF club, perhaps). To gauge your strengths, take our BRIEF Communication Assessment Survey (BCAS) at thebrieflab.scoreapp.com/p/the-brief-lab.

**Create weekly tasks and challenges.** Apply what you have learned in the BRIEF courses and want to put into practice. Take four to six weeks as a team to apply dedicated quiet time to tighten your communication. Work on one area of focus each week. Further below, you'll see an example of a five-week program you can follow, which closely mirrors some of the work we do in the Quiet Works for BRIEF Teams course.

**Together, start changing the conversation.** As you tackle the challenges below, talk with your team about what is working for you and what's not. Are you setting and holding your appointments for quiet time? If not, why? If so, how? The beauty of working in a team is that everyone supports and learns from each other, and together you all become better.

## Five Weeks to Better Communication Using the Power of Quiet

Now that you've got your team, you can start a journey toward better communication using quiet, the missing ingredient. Here is a sample schedule that closely resembles the Quiet Works for BRIEF Teams coursework. Follow this guide or contact us to enroll your group in the course.

**Week One: Better meeting agendas and better meeting notes.** Take fifteen minutes to devise and revise an agenda for an upcoming meeting. Use your fifteen minutes to drill down on the core purpose of the meeting, look at the attendees and think about what they each have to offer and what they need from the meeting, review past action items, fine-tune the order and organization of the agenda, and establish a minimum definition of success.

Alternatively, take ten minutes to review the notes from a meeting you just completed. Transfer your notes into a BRIEF Map to create a better recap. Ask your team: What were the key issues we covered? What are our next steps?

**Week Two: Project and status updates.** Let's say at the end of each week you must give a project status update. Use thirty minutes of quiet to figure out the essential information you need to relay. Organize it, making sure you are sharing the appropriate levels of information with the appropriate people.

**Week Three: Better emails and text messages and better use of project management tools.** Before you send a Slack or text message, take two minutes of quiet to think before you write. Take five minutes before typing an email to write a few notes about what you want to say. Remember the T.O.W.E.R. method (the one we developed at The BRIEF Lab to encourage concise writers): always *think, outline, write, edit,* and *rewrite,* then hit send. If it's a shorter message, still take time to think before writing, reviewing, and revising, and then hit send.

**Week Four: One-on-one conversations.** Take a closer look at the many kinds of conversations you have this week—sidebars, drive-bys, spontaneous chats, planned phone calls. Start to practice preparing these in advance. If you have an upcoming call on Thursday, what do you want to say? Why is this phone call important (for all people involved)? For those shorter conversations, think about how you can make them more meaningful—what information will you convey, and what questions should you ask?

**Week Five: Audience adaptation.** Spend time in silence thinking about the many people you will be speaking in front of before you start communicating with them. For example, your boss, your clients, your peers. Who are these people? What makes them tick? Why are they important to you? How often do you need to talk to them, and why? Is the relationship strong, or could it be stronger?

When you've got quiet time scheduled, you will do it. It's an appointment you will keep because it's on your calendar. And that all-important quiet will finally enable you to use the methodology that you already know so well. Together, everyone in your group will create a sea change that shifts the organizational culture to one of BRIEF communication. The new communication will be refined, organized, clear, relevant, and, most of all, *impactful*.

## A BRIEF Lab Coach's Perspective: Part II

### All Time Is *Not* Created Equal

I had just finished teaching a course at The BRIEF Lab when I asked the participants a question I always ask: "What were some of your key insights?" One of the participants said, "I just realized that all time is not created equal. Five minutes of quiet is a long time. Five minutes on Facebook is nothing."

Wow, she nailed it! Quiet time is potent. You don't need a lot of it to make a big impact on your preparation. Even five minutes daily can start changes that make bigger impacts down the road. And everyone can find five minutes in a day to give quiet a chance. In fact, when you are paying attention, you'll notice plenty of opportunities for a dose of silence.

There's a lot to be said for paying attention. I'm reminded of my godfather, who only lived sixty years and died early from cancer. He was an amazing person who lived in the moment and gave so much of himself to the world because he was present. He lived more in sixty years than many people would in a hundred.

Quiet—even in small doses—can introduce the kind of presence my godfather had to the rest of us. Time may not all be equal, but you can make your quiet time count.

Finally, if you're waiting around for those thirty or forty-five minutes when you feel really fresh, focused, calm, and ready to prepare, stop. No one can afford to wait for all the planets to line up. This kind of inspirational jolt does happen occasionally, but it's rare to get a big window of time when you're ready *and* able to prepare for that upcoming meeting or phone call or sales pitch. Seize the (quiet) moment. This is really about taking (and making) little pockets of time and using them to their fullest potential. And when you're not distracted or disrupted by screens and other people, that little chunk of time becomes significant.

## A Snapshot of Success: Being Prepared and Being Brief

There's never been a better time to make a change. Do you really want to keep rushing from one meeting to the next and thinking of what you'll say two seconds before you jump on a call? Being chronically underprepared isn't a satisfying way to work or live. Instead of feeling rushed and anxious, your life could look something like this:

- Yesterday, I prepped for today's call with an analyst. I feel focused and ready.
- I need to check in with my team in thirty minutes and I have prepared by looking at the notes from our last meeting. I am up to speed and ready to lead the meeting.
- I need to send an important email to my boss. I used quiet to consider what I want to say and how I want to say it.

This is what success looks like when you make being prepared a priority. It might be a huge contrast from what you're used to, but it makes your work, your communication, and your life so much more enjoyable—and it makes you a pleasure to work with, too.

## A BRIEF Lab Coach's Perspective: Part III

### The Missing Ingredient That Makes the Difference

After yet another training session, I asked the team to share what they had learned. One person said to me, "I was surprised by how much taking a little bit of quiet affected me physiologically throughout the day." She described how her heart rate would be higher on days she didn't have quiet time. This is because quiet is a little thing, but when you skip it, it completely changes the outcome you get. It's like adding yeast to the dough that makes a loaf of bread. You could skip it, but you would end up with a different outcome. It's the same way with quiet. Don't skip the yeast. Don't skip the quiet.

When you're looking at the big picture, it becomes clear that people who use quiet get more use out of their time. The impact of this goes far beyond their professional lives. They live more because they are living purposefully and intentionally in the present. It's a big idea, but it's really simple to execute.

You might think this sounds so far from where you are starting now that it will be impossible to achieve. It's not. You might have an uphill push ahead of you to get rid of bad habits and stick to your quiet, but remember that each small intentional step will eventually get you where you want to go. It's time to become an elite communicator, and quiet will get you there.

For more information, check out the *Just Saying* podcast, episode "Quiet Works for BRIEF Teams": podcast.thebrieflab.com/ep-303.

## BRIEFLY STATED

Quiet is the missing ingredient that makes the difference in our communication—for individuals and teams. With the clear, methodical plan of Quiet Works for BRIEF Teams, everyone learns from each other and benefits as a group.

## QUIET CONSIDERATIONS

**DO I:** feel the stress of jumping from meeting to meeting, from email to email, from Slack message to Slack message, without time for quiet reflection and planning?

**WOULD I:** benefit from challenging myself to add the regimen of Quiet Works for BRIEF Teams to enhance my already familiar BRIEF toolbox?

**CAN I:** convince my team to get on board to consistently work together through the Quiet Works for BRIEF Team course to start our journey toward quiet and concise communication?

# Chapter 20

# An Essay: Imagining the Quiet Workplace

L et's back up a little so I can share more about the inspiration for the book you're reading today—and the moment I first envisioned what a quiet workplace could look and feel like.

It was spring of 2021 and the whole world had just powered through a life-altering pandemic. People had been stuck at home for what felt like ages. Some had moved to new towns or cities to get a fresh start. Some moved to bigger houses to accommodate their new work-from-home life-style. And for many, COVID-19 was a wake-up call: millions of employees quit their jobs and set out in search of more rewarding work. (Of course, there were also plenty of quiet quitters, too. And I *don't* mean the kind of "quiet" this book is about—I mean those disillusioned employees who are resigned to doing the minimum amount of work to collect a paycheck.)

In other words, the pandemic overturned everything we once accepted about the workplace and how we work. Suddenly, the future was up for grabs. Some people believed people would (and should) return to the office full-time, while others envisioned a completely remote professional workforce. The truth was no one really knew what would happen.

But the question of the future of work got me thinking, and soon an idea took root. I felt strongly that the workplace needed to be reimagined because, like it or not, work and people were changing in fundamental ways. A twenty-three-year-old college graduate in 2024 will have very different expectations than a professional who graduated even five years earlier. Younger generations are growing more vocal about their preferences—when they work, how they work, where they work, and how they want to be led.

And then I wondered: What if there was a way that everyone could have exactly what they needed to do great work? The silence of their home office *and* the community of a workplace. Autonomy over their day *and* the support of leaders close at hand. Time to think *and* time to write, speak, and act.

In a moment of inspiration (during my quiet time, of course), I sat down with my pen.

And here is what I wrote:

## The Quiet Workplace: An Essay

Every morning, I dread my morning commute. It's not the traffic or time wasted so much as what awaits me once I finally get there.

It's not the people, really. They're nice, welcoming, and usually helpful.

You see, there's so much careless movement, undirected action, useless words, and pointless posturing. My mind immediately and constantly races to find something to latch onto to gauge where I'm supposed to be going, only to see myself and others chasing our tails more frequently than heading forward. My brain starts feeling the incessant abuse of a barrage of noise that I can never get to clarify or direct but only gets more distracted and divided.

The environment is far from quiet.

I don't mean one of pure silence like a library, but one filled with energy, purpose—and pauses. If work were equated to going on journey, there would be a similarly appropriate amount of time set aside for planning, rest, and recovery, not just always trudging along. Because that is what we do. When there's a cacophony of activity, we trudge along and equate that with moving forward. When it's not quiet, we never stop to look back at the wasted efforts invested in our twists and turns, and we rarely look far enough forward to set our sights on what's better, different, or next.

When the environment is not quiet, we don't ask questions. We just keep on talking and walking. And that takes a toll on me.

I feel frustrated more than fulfilled, and it's tiring. I may want to leave where I work, but I'm stuck. Where would I go, anyway? Home or to a park? Take a long walk? Maybe, but what if my workplace gave me a different space?

A place to think a little or a lot . . . not somewhere that's basically thoughtless.

A place where I could feel a sense of balance, connection, and purpose . . . not corporate callousness.

A place where I could often do what's challenging and meaningful . . . not what's useless.

That would sound great to me. That would sound less like the droning of a loud machine. That would really sound more like a rhythmic, melodic hum. Much more human, way more humane.

That would be a Quiet Workplace, and I would love heading there every day!

I looked at the essay that had just flowed so freely from my heart and mind. My vision for a Quiet Workplace was so starkly different from what

I had seen in nearly every organization I had been involved with up to that point. People weren't getting what they needed to be productive, creative, and clear and concise when communicating their thoughts and ideas. A big reason for that is the physical layout of their offices.

## The Open Floor Plan Fiasco

One of the big questions we've talk about in this book is, "Where do I go for quiet?" Everything I teach in these pages depends on you having a physical place to go where no one will bother you. People who have private offices are lucky in this regard. (Though they would be the first to tell you that having a door doesn't equate to having quiet—not when anyone can barge in to chat any time.) But for the rest of us, finding a place to routinely step away into for some boundaries between us and our coworkers remains a problem.

That's because most organizations today use open-concept office spaces. Over the years, private offices have been replaced by large rooms of desks with few or no dividing walls between them. The idea was to give people more opportunities to collaborate, improve the culture, and cut down on costs. But it has also resulted in people struggling to focus and get their work done.

These offices are full of noise, both literally and figuratively. People must work harder than ever to tune it out. There are no rules of engagement, and coworkers can disrupt each other any time. Maybe some can find a quiet nook where they can get some peace or use their trusty Do Not Disturb signs to remind others to keep it down. But in open offices, everyone knows the noise is nearly impossible to banish entirely.

Some companies have tried to jerry-rig solutions for quiet. They might designate a quiet conference room for whispered conversations or no talking. Others provide nap pods. Or they designate office-wide quiet hours. These implementations aren't necessarily bad, but neither are they real, lasting solutions. Not everyone needs or wants a nap at work—they just want to get their work done. And who says the office's quiet hours suit your schedule and workload?

When I ask people what they need to do their work, they always describe the same problem. They say they have no place to go in their office to focus. Maybe they can do it at home, they admit. If their kids, pets, and partner stay out of the way.

None of these workarounds work particularly well over the long haul. Wouldn't it be nice if professionals had somewhere they could reliably go for silence and focus?

> **For more information, check out the *Just Saying* podcast, episode "The Failure of Open Floor Plans": podcast.thebrieflab .com/episode-61-the-failure-of-open-floor-plans.**

## The Quiet Workplace Comes to Life

Inspired by this question, and full of ideas that had been percolating from the moment I penned my essay, I continued envisioning what the Quiet Workplace would look and feel like in real life. Before I knew it, a breathtaking picture started forming in my mind. I knew I was onto something big. If I could help organizations embody the quiet principles we covered back in chapter nine through their culture, their practices, and the physical layouts of their offices, the Quiet Workplace could go from dream to reality.

Here's a simple snapshot of what this utopian work environment could look like:

Employees arrive at work full of creative energy and ready for the day ahead. The atmosphere is calm and relaxed, punctuated occasionally with pleasant conversation and lighthearted laughter. No one feels tense or stressed because everyone, from junior employees to the most senior leaders, knows that here, attention is respected and protected.

People settle into their workspaces and a hush falls over the room as everyone begins their daily tasks. Even those without a private office have options for the times they want or need solitary focus. The office features personal workspaces similar to study carrels in a library that people can occupy anytime for uninterrupted quiet. Comfortable and cozy, these private areas are the perfect retreat. But even when workers choose to stay at their regular workstations, they use Do Not Disturb signs asking others for silence—and their colleagues gladly comply.

Not only do employees enjoy breaks from human noise, but they also take time-outs from digital noise. They regularly close their laptops, silence their phones, and enjoy a low-tech morning or afternoon. It's not uncommon to see an employee scribbling away on a notepad to capture a brilliant idea. Workers even occasionally lean back and close their eyes for a five- or ten-minute "brain break." Leaders understand that the mind needs rest, even during the workday, and they encourage employees to take the time they need to refresh and recharge their energy.

As the day unfolds, employees are free to come and go as they so choose. Some work in the office full-time, while hybrid employees spend certain days working on-site and others working from home. Leaders give employees the autonomy to do what works best for them because productivity and work quality are at all-time highs. They don't raise an eyebrow if employees block out plenty of white space on their calendars for quiet time, including before and after meetings. On the contrary, leaders encourage employees to spend time organizing their thoughts before client and coworker interactions.

And speaking of collaboration: meetings of all kinds are well planned and well executed. Employees who come together have prepared ahead of time, which helps them be clear, concise communicators. (There are plenty of spaces for meetings to take place, so as to not disturb other colleagues: conference rooms for group collaboration, private areas for smaller groups, and relaxing spaces for casual chats.)

In the Quiet Workplace, meetings are of the highest caliber. Leaders are able to see the big picture and empower employees to work hard to reach their company's goals. Likewise, employees understand what is being asked of them and can give their best performance. After converging for efficient and effective collaboration, everyone disperses to continue their quiet work.

Everyone operates on a higher level in the Quiet Workplace. Introverts and extroverts alike thrive, enjoying something closer to balance than they have ever experienced before. Employees achieve their peak performance. Leaders help the organization become more successful, and shareholders are satisfied and happy. True to the vision I put forth in my essay, the workplace finally becomes more human and much more humane. And yes, all professionals love heading there every day.

## The First Quiet Workplace

I set out to design such a space in Southern Pines, North Carolina. Or rather, to *redesign* the workplace in a way that works for everyone. It wasn't just a matter of designing offices with doors, but rather designing spaces for different types of work. It would need open spaces for collaboration, small conference rooms for focused discussion, and private, dedicated, guarded sections for quiet work done alone.

I thought deeply about what I wanted this space to be. I researched and then fabricated prototype workspaces. I tested them and fine-tuned every aspect of the experience.

The Quiet Workplace would be segregated and secure so that noise cannot overflow into the quiet areas. It would be the combination of a library, gym, and airport lounge where you go with one thing in mind: to work quietly alone, without fear of distractions or disruptions.

Soon my vision started taking shape. Here are some features of the Quiet Workplace:

**Designed for quiet.** Truly quiet workplaces just don't exist in offices on their own. You have to make them. The Quiet Workplace has been designed to intentionally mask all noises and create a calming, comfortable atmosphere. It features a white noise system to ensure you don't hear your neighbors next door. And the reservation system operates through an app for voiceless entry.

**A proprietary reservation system to check in and out *by yourself.*** With the Quiet Works reservation application, you can set an appointment for quiet. The app allows for a contactless check-in experience and sends you to an individual space reserved just for you.

**Thresholds to silence.** The reception area is a "sacred" space designed to help you transition into a period of quiet. Similar to the entrance to a church's sanctuary, it prepares you for the work ahead. It's not just a place; it's a mindset that will help you quickly find your focus. The peaceful lobby is designed to create a threshold to silence. It is a boundary between the collaborative workspace and the quiet workspace, separating two distinct areas. It is like the entrance to a spa, an airport lounge, or a library and breaks the two spaces apart so the client knows they are entering a quiet space.

**Individual quiet workspaces.** The first thing I conceptualized was the design of the individual work areas. I was reminded of first and business class airplane seats one encounters when flying overseas, and I also drew inspiration from the study carrels I would frequent in the stacks of the library at my college whenever I needed to put my head down and focus.

Each unit feels like you're in a small office and an airline pod at the same time. The spaces have a large, comfortable leather chair, a small desk with a chair, dimmable lighting, and two dry-erase boards. They also include a timer, indicating when your quiet time is ending, while also allowing you to extend your time if space is available.

**Training through simple, practical experiences.** Everything about the Quiet Workplace is geared to train you to become a quiet professional. From our patented layout to our trained quiet professional enforcing our standards of silence, it is an integrated system to ensure that people stop talking. Remember, the urge to speak is very strong in us humans, so we actually need training to ensure we don't perpetuate noise with our voices. There are orientation sessions on expected behaviors, in which participants are reminded that this is a place of "no tech or low tech," that they shouldn't distract others, and not to worry about doing quiet time perfectly. Little to no policing is needed when people know and follow the standards of behavior. Secondly, since the idea of sustained quiet may initially seem long or awkward, we train people to plan for it, encouraging them to consider in advance how they intend to use their time well. Lastly, we encourage them to connect with how we use Quiet Workplace training to prepare to be a BRIEF communicator and follow the mantra of Think, Speak, Do once they cross back to the collaborative world.

**Managed staffing services.** The Quiet Workplace has trained quiet professionals to protect the quiet standards and ensure you become a quiet professional yourself. Again, the urge to speak and disrupt others is strong. To ensure the environment is always quiet, we provide a dedicated, trained staff to ensure people don't talk—ever. They are not attendants but coaches, counselors, and facilitators that believe deeply in the brand promise and play a vigilant role for you to use the space and find different ways to benefit from it.

On a practical level, I think that the workplace needs to be broken into two parts. One should be designed for collaboration, communication, and connections, where ideas flow freely and professionals interact with purpose and passion. The other would be separate, a place where people can go to be alone in quiet to think, plan, read, decide, and determine new paths. These spaces need to be near each other but segregated and protected so that when a professional needs to step out of a connected environment, they can confidently go into a quiet space without fear of someone following or interrupting them. The back-and-forth movement between these environments is the key to do fulfilling and meaningful work because work is both collaboration and concentration. It's time together and time alone.

Workspaces, therefore, need to be significantly redesigned and reimagined in this way. Trying to isolate people to do quiet work within a noisy and open space won't work. It makes people look and feel out of place, disconnected, and disinterested; it actually makes them look like fish out of water.

When I reimagine workspaces like this, I see several powerful use cases for it:

- **Day-to-day refuges.** Organizations providing dedicated spaces for their employees to go to during the workday by making reservations for set times.
- **Quiet Workplace memberships.** Individual professionals and companies buying memberships (like a gym or airport club) to utilize during the week.
- **Building amenities.** Owners of buildings providing dedicated Quiet Workplaces that attract new tenants into their buildings.
- **Quiet off-site locations.** Spaces for teams to go to for a day or two to think alone and collaborate together.

Giving people a dedicated place for quiet is better than just talking about it.

Since these spaces do not exist, owners, tenants, and organizations would need to finance them into new space designs. Each of these use cases is a powerful, real, and practical application of the desperate need for quiet. Like in the movie *Field of Dreams*, the adage "if you build it, they will come" rings true.

To learn more, visit thequietworkplace.com.

As workplaces continue to evolve, everyone needs refuge from the noise. Modern offices currently don't provide this, which is why every professional has experienced disruption regardless of all the ways they signal to others that they are busy. Whether or not you decide to use the Quiet Workplace model, it's crucial to design a space to mitigate the noise and disruption that keeps employees from their focus and to make the office a more pleasant and productive place to be.

Which brings me to the big question. What does the future of work look like for professionals?

I predict that the future of work is hybrid. Some people will continue working from home with their employers' blessing. Some will join teams in the office full-time. But a vast majority, I believe, will do some of both. We have already seen this play out in many organizations nationwide, and as we find our "new normal," its likely that more workplaces will become hybrid. If my prediction is correct, this means that organizations will need to sweeten the pot. Luring people with foosball tables, in-office bars, gyms, or naps anytime is not the way. There's a time and a place for fun and leisure, but professionals want to feel productive and maintain some level of autonomy. It's up to leaders to help them do just that. They need a compelling reason to return to in-person work—even on a part-time basis.

Entice them with quiet, and they will come back.

*Quiet* is what they love about working from home. *Quiet* is what they crave when they come to the office. A Quiet Workplace is a win-win for everyone. Employees get what they need to do their jobs well, and employers can collaborate and meet with their employees face-to-face when needed. It's a refuge that we deeply need. And it can continue bringing people together again.

## BRIEFLY STATED

Expectations for the workplace have drastically changed over the past few years, with some people choosing to work at home and some craving in-person contact and collaboration. To meet these conflicting expectations, the workspace needs to be reimagined and redesigned, with places for both quiet and community. The Quiet Workplace is the solution.

## QUIET CONSIDERATIONS

**DO I:** get frustrated by constant interruptions and noise during my workday?

**WOULD I:** benefit from a thoughtfully redesigned workspace where I can go to focus on deep work in true quiet?

**CAN I:** successfully merge my planned quiet time with more purposeful collaboration time by incorporating the Quiet Workplace model?

# PART FIVE

# QUIET CHALLENGES

It's critical to experience quiet in small, specific, and deliberate ways to stop avoiding it during the day. We need to challenge ourselves and each other to "do nothing" in order to realize that this absence of noisy, busy work is actually something. Each challenge we embrace gives us a chance to discover, fail, learn, and lead ourselves and others out of mindless, thoughtless bad working habits and create new occasions for clarity, consistency, and purpose that put us back in charge.

# Chapter 21

# Professional Leaders Predict a Payoff—QCO: Questions, Challenges, and Observations

During my years in business in my roles as a marketing executive, facilitator, instructor, or consultant, I always found that asking people, "Do you have any questions?" rarely led to many questions. So, several years ago, I created a prompt called "QCO" to get people talking. What I decided to do was give people two minutes of quiet to write down any questions, challenges, or observations they had. I encouraged everyone to use that moment of silence to write something—anything—down. That little trick (strategy?) always sparks a conversation.

While I was finishing the manuscript for this book, I decided to reach out to my extended network to get them thinking more about what a future that included predictable times and places for silence would look like. I fielded a simple survey called "The Future of Work: Does Quiet Fit In?" As the book winds down, this chapter includes an amalgam of their QCO responses.

## Questions

The surveyed professionals had a variety of questions ranging from logistics to more philosophical issues. We can't solve all their problems, but here are some responses to their outlying queries:

- **Question**: "How can we encourage leadership to provide time and places for quiet? 'Alone' work could tend to be territorial, and organizations that want groupthink and groupspeak won't like it."
  - **Answer**: First, tell them that you need it. Then, respectfully ask them: What is the cost of a workforce that's not provided times and places to think in quiet alone at work? The answer is that they're letting their people devalue being intentional during working hours.
- **Question:** "How can we fight the perception that you lose connectivity with the customer if you aren't reachable 24/7 (something everyone promotes as a standard of business these days)?"
  - **Answer:** I think that off hours need to be part of the customer conversation, getting them to agree to letting certain hours and dates be off limits (that aren't real emergencies).
- **Question:** "When is the last time that an interviewer asked a job candidate if they can work well alone?"
  - **Answer:** It's been far too long. Today the question is always "How well do you work with others on a team?" Managers have been brainwashed to think that silence is counterproductive. But candidates need to be asked about their ability to work alone, knowing their managers value uninterrupted thinking and need to encourage and promote it.
- **Question:** "How can an organization convince people—from all generations—that quiet is a priority and help them to develop the discipline to practice it?"
  - **Answer:** I think that what needs to be promoted is a balance

between two types of work: one done together with connection and collaboration, and another where quiet time alone is essential. It's an "and," not an "or," that creates a powerful combination, not competition.

- **Question:** "How can we balance the conflict between scheduled meetings with agendas passed out beforehand and this practice creating work required—between meetings—that forces collaboration/coordination at inopportune times?"
  - **Answer:** There's a time and place for everything, and there need to be boundaries. Much of the time, it comes down to setting some rules and enforcing them. Go back to the Covey Matrix to determine the importance of the issue and ask yourself, "Am I ready for collaboration? Is it a good time? How much time will it take?" Don't say yes right away. See if you can put some rules into unscheduled collaboration and have more control over the timeline.

- **Question:** "How can we overcome management having a lack of interest in setting/enforcing a new policy and get away from the stereotypical excuse of 'this is the way we've always done it'? How do we counter a lack of understanding that you can, indeed, have both collaboration and deep quiet?"
  - **Answer:** Start the conversation with them that work is both a collaborative process and an individual one. Get them to see that the more people are protected, the more they're productive.

## Challenges

When categorizing a lack of quiet in the workplace as being an issue of time, environment, or culture, 60 percent of people said that culture was the biggest problem, followed by environment (23 percent). The majority of respondents said they have the time for quiet but that the organization thinks and acts differently in terms of environment and behavior.

Here are some of the challenges professionals face at work:

- Nearly 70 percent of current work arrangements are hybrid.
- Almost 60 percent of professionals surveyed did not feel the current work environment had a proper balance between collaboration and quiet.
- Fewer than 65 percent of those surveyed schedule time for quiet every workday.
- The top five greatest sources of noise in the current work environment are:
  - meetings;
  - digital devices;
  - emails;
  - texting/instant messaging;
  - interruptions from coworkers/clients.
- "It would help greatly if there was the established environment and culture for [quiet]. [This would give] everyone 'permission' and social safety to do it."
- "It [a commitment to provide a time or place to do deep work alone] takes discipline and buy-in, attributes most organizations lack."
- "The biggest challenge would be to be able to explain to coworkers and management personnel that you will be unavailable during the 'scheduled' quiet times."
- "The problem is reliability in protecting the time for quiet. Easy to protect a meeting. Hard to protect something involving just you."
- "There is little respect for boundaries of a closed door, an unanswered text, or email. Expectations are for quick responses and interruptions do not allow for respected quiet reflective time."

## Observations

Not surprisingly, the biggest payoffs, if quiet time were a predictable part of the workday, revolved around fewer distractions, less stress, more productivity, and more focused thought.

Here are a few of the surveyed observations:

- "I find quiet time essential for strategy building and planning. Too many distractions and interruptions tend to make my thoughts fragmented at times."
- "I equate this to 3M's allotment of time for thinking of new ideas. When you promote quiet time, you're expressing its value—free your mind, stay focused, no interruptions. When management promotes it, there is no longer guilt or a stigma of not being a team player when you want to work alone."
- "From a daily perspective, carving out quiet time means clearing your plate from that day, so activities are promptly retired and don't 'snowball' into the week."
- "If I had [a work environment that promoted intentional collaboration with dedicated time to work alone in quiet], that would help my creativity, my nervous system, my efficiency, my mental health, and more."
- "[Quiet time] allows dedicated time to focus on what matters to *you*. Not just personal concerns, but *your* assigned project, or your professional *passions* ... both benefit the company. Allows you to invest/integrate with others, knowing you have dedicated time to address your needs."
- "Production would go up as long as there were not meetings about the meetings."
- "[Quiet time] would help me better focus on projects requiring some creative thought and structure. Bottom line, it would make me more productive."

---

As we begin the conversation about the role of quiet in the workplace, we will face obstacles. As the saying goes, "if it were easy, everybody would be doing it." What's encouraging to note is that when you start talking about it, professionals speak up. They really need it, yet many don't know to ask for it. When the opportunity is presented, however, very few say they love the nonstop noise, constant disruptions, and distractions to rule their day. They'd love to see a new reality and invite change.

So let's talk about not talking so much. Let's give professionals some peace and quiet, not another text, drive-by conversation, or long meeting. It's what they all need to get work done and feel fulfilled doing it!

## Chapter 22

# Challenges to Get You Started

As you've read throughout the book, taking time for quiet needs to be treated as something practical and achievable, not elusive or unrealistic. When working with professionals, I always challenge them to start with low-hanging fruit. The problem with many people is that they don't grab it, yet they reach for what's beyond their current capacity. Start small. Take a few steps. Fall and get back up.

I've designed seven challenges that I've done myself. None of them is impossible and all of them will help you create daily habits to be more intentional. Give them a chance, and you'll make progress quickly.

### Getting in the Habit

A day and week of quiet starts with you making a decision. To help you get in the habit of quiet, here are a series of simple and practical challenges to integrate throughout your workday. There are seven practices for seven days—one for each day of the week.

1. **One Minute of Quiet.** Quiet habits start when you give yourself permission to pause, even if it's only for sixty seconds.

   *Instructions*: Set a timer for one minute, stop what you were doing, and simply be in silence. Once the minute is over, give yourself another minute (or two) to write down what you thought, felt, heard, experienced, etc.

   *Considerations*: Each of us can experience time in different ways depending on many factors. During your minute of silence, you may want to experiment with the time(s) of the day you do it or even what you were doing or where you were. Sitting, walking, or standing up can all lead to different experiences. Then note how and when your minute of quiet is most impactful.

2. **Quiet Time AM/PM.** Set the tone for the entire day with ten minutes of quiet first thing in the morning or last thing in the day (or both!).

   *Instructions*: When you wake up, instead of grabbing your phone, grab a cup of coffee or favorite drink and sit down with a pen and paper in a quiet space. Set a timer for ten minutes and reflect on the day's priorities, both personal and professional. Define your minimum definition of success and write down any important things you need to set aside for quiet.

   *Considerations*: First, think about your current morning routine and where you can invest some time. If you hate to wake earlier, you can do the challenge the night before.

   Second, you may be tempted to write a laundry list of to-dos. Don't. Instead of overwhelming yourself with a list of tasks that may or may not get crossed off throughout the day, reflect on three to five most important things that require your valuable attention. Examples:
   - Task or to-do that you need some deep work in solitude to complete

– Key decision you need to reflect on or make

– An upcoming appointment or conversation

Helpful tools to use could be a journal or planner. You can also purchase our Quiet Works Planner at thequietworkplace .com/store.

3. **Distraction Tracker.** Start to notice who and what might be stealing your valuable attention from meaningful work.

*Instructions*: When you sit down to work, keep a running tally of the drive-bys and "Hey, you" encounters. Note every time someone asks, "Do you have a sec?" or when someone expects you to drop everything you're doing for their "emergency." Think about when you do this yourself as well. At the end of the day, tally up who and what are the greatest disruptions to your day.

Over time, think about some solutions to reduce the noise like those you've read thus far. If it's a particular person or group, would it help to set up a weekly check-in? Can you reduce the distractions by turning off notifications or by finding a quieter space? Are there standard criteria for what constitutes an emergency across the team?

*Considerations*:

– Working remotely? Note the "urgent" emails and messages and unplanned meetings or calls.

– Working at the office? Note every time someone drops by your desk unannounced or corners you for an unplanned conversation.

– Is it really an emergency? If you're wondering if the distraction is urgent, it probably isn't. There's nothing wrong with saying, "No, not now."

4. **Reclaim a Space.** Do you have a quiet place where you can think and get deep work done without disruption or distraction? Designating a specific location for quiet is essential to maintaining the habit of daily quiet time.

*Instructions*: Whether working remotely or at the office, designate a space where you can work without being disturbed. Let others know it's your quiet space, and post signs if needed to discourage disruptors.

*Considerations*: You may need to get creative. If you work at a cubicle-topia or in an open office plan, reserving an empty room or posting Do Not Disturb signs around your workspace are great ways to discourage others from disrupting you. For ideas or signage, you can visit our site at thequietworkplace.com.

5. **Take 5.** When we have important things to do, people to see, or places to go, we schedule time for them. But have you ever scheduled a short appointment that's less than thirty minutes? Scheduling five minutes of nonnegotiable quiet helps you use slices of an hour productively.

   *Instructions*: Pick a topic/task you can do in silence for five minutes (e.g., plan, choose, prepare, reflect, etc.). Set a timer and quietly embrace that single consideration for only five minutes. During the time, write down or mentally note what comes to mind. Schedule these mini appointments a few times a day during pockets of free time.

   *Considerations*: Stumped for something to do during your five minutes? You can make a list ahead of time of simple tasks to choose from (e.g., read, study, pray, dream). You can also choose a topic from a deck of Take 5 Cards from thequietworkplace.com/store.

   Struggling to find the time? Intentionally schedule the five minutes on your calendar or begin looking for opportunities:
   - When a meeting ends early, or as you are waiting for another one to begin
   - During your commute
   - A coffee or bathroom break
   - While taking a longer route to walk to your meeting, breakroom, or car

6.  **Quiet Meeting Insert.** Five minutes of quiet can turn a meeting from pandemonium to productive.

    *Instructions*: Start to implement quiet at any time during a meeting by setting a timer or designating someone to start a timer. Decide what amount of quiet time is appropriate for your team and the meeting length. One minute of quiet might be all that's feasible for a fifteen- to thirty-minute meeting, whereas five minutes may be a better fit for a one-hour meeting. Then give participants a purpose for the quiet time (i.e., review the agenda, reflect, prepare questions, etc.).

    *Considerations*:
    -   But what if you're not the one in charge? You may not be able to instigate a group-wide moment of silence, but you can have your own private moment. Take a few minutes before you go into a meeting to pause, reflect, and organize your thoughts.
    -   Coming from back-to-back meetings? Have silence at the beginning of the meeting so everyone can regroup or review the read-ahead.
    -   Is the meeting descending into chaos? Or do the participants need to make a vote? Institute a quiet time-out to allow attendees to reflect and organize their thoughts.
    -   You can make quiet a standard for every meeting your team has (e.g., institute five minutes of quiet at the beginning of every meeting without technology).

7.  **7-to-7.** We are constantly checking our digital devices all day—and night! In a survey, 70 percent of respondents admitted that the first and last thing they do every day is to check their phone.[1] By placing boundaries on technology and blocking out time (i.e., 7 PM to 7 AM), we start to recognize that technology is a choice—not a necessary constant.

    *Instructions*: Pick a set time in the evening and in the morning to disconnect from all digital devices. For that time period, do not check them (although you can leave them on in case there's an emergency). Put all the devices far enough from where you sleep to hear but not use them. Set this "7-to-7" time period as off hours for several days.

*Considerations*: Adapt the challenge to work for you. The time and location you put devices in should work with your routine. For example, some families have found it helpful to put all devices in a basket or box once everyone gets home for the day. Others have purchased an analog alarm clock to help wake them up so they aren't reaching for their phones first thing in the morning.

## Moving Forward

The challenges are not intended to be prescriptive but rather to be adapted to best support your life and schedule. You can attempt one per day or compound them over time to determine which practices are the most helpful to reducing the noise.

Please always keep in mind that silence is the secret ingredient of every workday. It's what's been missing, so don't fail to include it.

Remember, the book title is also the promise: quiet works!

# Acknowledgments

Quiet is a gift I've received, and I'm so grateful for it. Writing this book has been richly rewarding because I now get to share that gift openly with many others.

To me, writing this book seemed to be a logical continuation to writing *NOISE: Living and Leading When Nobody Can Focus* five years ago. After finishing chapter fourteen of that book, "Quiet Time: Restoring and Recharging Your Mind," I started a journey of trying to practice what I preached—each small step leading me one step forward.

There are several people I want to thank for helping me along the way.

From the very beginning, my wife, Julie, believed in the vision and value of what I was describing to her incessantly as the future of work. Her love, encouragement, and belief in me has been present every day.

Because there were two previous books, I wanted the cover design to be consistent in look and feel to them so they'd all be seen as one family (because they are). Alison Hall helped translate my vague artistic direction into a cover design that kept a Quiet Works brand intact and beautiful. Karen Quinn, who helped me with *NOISE*, was again an invaluable friend, resource, and editor, leading Sam Hayes with research and keeping me on schedule.

## Acknowledgments

Matt Holt and his team at BenBella have been amazing partners from day one. Their attention to detail and comprehensive support have been a critical element to getting the word out on how quiet works to the world.

My coworkers and colleagues continue to believe in me and the vision of bringing clarity to work at the Sheffield Company through The BRIEF Lab and Quiet Works programs. Most notably, Jamie Moses, Charley Thornton, John Nutt, and Jeff Hutchinson helped in several chapters that detail select programs targeted to our clients. Our marketing team of Michelle O'Hagan, Pat Reilly, Michelle McKinney, and Melissa Kohlman helped in so many creative and strategic ways.

Finally, I want to acknowledge the clients we support every day. Most noteworthy are the men and women of US Special Operations and their partner organizations that we serve through our programs. These quiet professionals value selflessness and excellence in all they do. I'm motivated to give them anything that gives them an advantage and makes them better. I am honored and grateful to be considered a trusted partner.

# *Notes*

## Chapter 2

1. Joe McCormack, "BRIEF FACT SHEET" (unpublished internal document), The BRIEF Lab, Southern Pines, NC, 2021.
2. Jen Fisher, "Workplace Burnout Survey: Burnout Without Borders," Deloitte, accessed February 15, 2024, https://www2.deloitte.com/us/en/pages/about-deloitte/articles/burnout-survey.html.
3. "Workplace Stress," American Institute of Stress, accessed February 15, 2024, https://www.stress.org/workplace-stress.
4. Rick Wartzman and Kelly Tang, "What Good Leadership Looks Like Now vs. Pre-Covid," *Wall Street Journal*, September 17, 2022, https://www.wsj.com/articles/what-good-leadership-looks-like-now-vs-pre-covid-11663180016.
5. Kate Rodriguez, "How Einstein and Edison Solved Problems in Their Sleep," *Inc.*, August 1, 2016, https://www.inc.com/the-muse/albert-einstein-thomas-edison-your-half-asleep-brain-can-solve-problems-better.html.
6. "Hybrid Work Is Just Work. Are We Doing It Wrong?" Microsoft, September 22, 2022, https://www.microsoft.com/en-us/worklab/work-trend-index/hybrid-work-is-just-work.

## Chapter 3

1. Ray A. Smith, "Workers Now Spend Two Full Days a Week on Email and in Meetings," *Wall Street Journal*, May 9, 2023, https://www.wsj.com/articles/workers-say-its-harder-to-get-things-done-now-heres-why-2a5f1389?mod=hp_listb_pos2.

# Notes

2. Dawn Klinghoffer and Elizabeth McCune, "Why Microsoft Measures Employee Thriving, Not Engagement," *Harvard Business Review*, June 24, 2022, https://hbr .org/2022/06/why-microsoft-measures-employee-thriving-not-engagement.

3. Rob Cross, "Where We Go Wrong with Collaboration," *Harvard Business Review*, April 4, 2022, https://hbr.org/2022/04/where-we-go-wrong-with-collaboration.

## Chapter 4

1. McCormack, "BRIEF FACT SHEET."

2. Emily Boynton, "Taking Breaks Is Good for Your Brain—Here's Why," Right as Rain by UW Medicine, April 18, 2022, https://rightasrain.uwmedicine.org/mind /well-being/taking-breaks.

## Chapter 5

1. Rakesh Kochhar, "Which U.S. Workers Are More Exposed to AI on Their Jobs?," Pew Research Center, July 26, 2023, https://www.pewresearch.org/social-trends/2023 /07/26/which-u-s-workers-are-more-exposed-to-ai-on-their-jobs/.

2. Ben Popken, "Manufacturers Embrace Robots, the Perfect Pandemic Worker," NBC News, April 8, 2021, https://www.nbcnews.com/business/business-news/manufacturers -embrace-robots-perfect-pandemic-worker-n1263434.

3. "Top Generative AI Statistics for 2023," Salesforce, September 2023, https://www .salesforce.com/news/stories/generative-ai-statistics/.

4. Smith, "Workers Now Spend Two Full Days a Week on Email and in Meetings."

## Chapter 7

1. Thomas Merton, *Thoughts in Solitude* (New York: Farrar, Straus and Giroux, 1999).

2. "The Privacy Crisis: Taking a Toll on Employee Engagement," Steelcase, accessed October 27, 2023, https://www.steelcase.com/research/articles/privacy-crisis/.

3. McCormack, "BRIEF FACT SHEET."

4. Donna McGeorge, "Find Focus with These 4 Tips to Reframe Time Management," *Forbes Australia*, March 7, 2023, https://www.forbes.com.au/news/leadership/find -focus-with-these-4-tips-to-reframe-time-management/.

## Chapter 8

1. E. T. Klemmer and F. W. Snyder, "Measurement of Time Spent Communicating," *Journal of Communication* 22, no. 2 (June 1972), doi:10.1111/j.1460-2466.1972.tb00141.x.

2. Owen Hargie, *Skilled Interpersonal Interaction: Research, Theory, and Practice*

(London: Routledge, 2011), 177, quoted in *Communication in the Real World: An Introduction to Communication Studies* (Twin Cities, MN: University of Minnesota Libraries Publishing, 2016), chapter 5, https://open.lib.umn.edu/communication /part/chapter-5-listening/.

## Chapter 12

1. Julia Martins, "Multitasking Doesn't Work—Here's What Does," Asana, December 15, 2022, https://asana.com/resources/multitasking.
2. Kermit Pattison, "Worker, Interrupted: The Cost of Task Switching," *Fast Company*, July 28, 2008, https://www.fastcompany.com/944128/worker-interrupted-cost -task-switching.

## Chapter 13

1. Simon Kemp, "Digital 2023: Global Overview Report," DataReportal, January 26, 2023, https://datareportal.com/reports/digital-2023-global-overview-report.
2. Ibid.
3. Ibid.
4. Brian Elliott, "Not All Daily Active Users Are Created Equal: Work Is Fueled by True Engagement," Slack (blog), October 10, 2019, https://slack.com/blog/news/work -is-fueled-by-true-engagement.
5. Federica Laricchia, "Average Number of Connected Devices in U.S. House-holds 2020," Statista, June 1, 2022, https://statista.com/statistics/1107206/average -number-of-connected-devices-us-house/.
6. Stephanie Chan, "U.S. Consumers Used an Average of 46 Apps Each Month in the First Half of 2021," Sensor Tower, August 2021, https://sensortower.com/blog/apps -used-per-us-smartphone.
7. Joseph McCormack, *NOISE: Living and Leading When Nobody Can Focus* (Hoboken, NJ: Wiley, 2019), 28.
8. Joe McCormack, "BRIEF Survey" (unpublished internal document), The BRIEF Lab, Southern Pines, NC, February 4, 2017.
9. Catherine Pearson, "The Insidious Habit That Can Hurt Your Relationship," *New York Times*, July 27, 2023, https://www.nytimes.com/2023/07/27/well/family/phubbing -phone-snubbing-relationship.html.
10. Michele W. Berger, "Social Media Use Increases Depression and Loneliness," Penn Today, November 9, 2018, https://penntoday.upenn.edu/news/social-media -use-increases-depression-and-loneliness.

Notes

. "Dealing with Devices: The Parent-Teen Dynamic," Common Sense Media, 2016, https://www.commonsensemedia.org/technology-addiction-concern-controversy-and-finding-balance-infographic.
12. Elia Abi-Jaoude, Karline Treurnicht Naylor, and Antonio Pignatiello, "Smartphones, Social Media Use and Youth Mental Health," *Canadian Medical Association Journal* 192, no. 6 (February 10, 2020): E136, doi:10.1503/cmaj.190434.
13. Lawrence Robinson and Melinda Smith, "Social Media and Mental Health," HelpGuide.org, March 29, 2023, https://www.helpguide.org/articles/mental-health/social-media-and-mental-health.htm.

## Chapter 14

1. Callum Borchers, "The New Workday Dead Zone When Nothing Gets Done," *Wall Street Journal*, July 16, 2023, https://www.wsj.com/articles/work-office-coworkers-schedule-meetings-2af3f9b0.
2. "The Rise of the Triple Peak Day," Microsoft, accessed February 15, 2024, https://www.microsoft.com/en-us/worklab/triple-peak-day.

## Chapter 15

1. Taylor Locke, "Jeff Bezos: This Is the 'Smartest Thing We Ever Did' at Amazon," CNBC, October 14, 2019, https://www.cnbc.com/2019/10/14/jeff-bezos-this-is-the-smartest-thing-we-ever-did-at-amazon.html.

## Chapter 17

1. "Membership and Credentialing Fact Sheet," International Coaching Federation, February 2021, https://coachingfederation.org/app/uploads/2021/02/February2021_FactSheet.pdf.
2. "International Coaching Federation Releases 2020 Global Coaching Study," International Coaching Federation, accessed February 15, 2024, https://coachingfederation.org/blog/international-coaching-federation-releases-2020-global-coaching-study.

## Chapter 22

1. Joe McCormack, "Sheffield Company LLC Survey" (unpublished internal document), Sheffield Company LLC, Southern Pines, NC, 2019.

## About Joe McCormack

Photo by Richard Barlow

Joe McCormack is passionate about helping professionals gain focus and clarity in a world of too much information, too much collaboration, and too much noise. As an entrepreneur, marketing executive, and author, he is recognized for his work in concise, strategic communication and leadership development.

In 2006, Joe founded the Sheffield Company (sheffieldcompany.com), a specialty marketing agency that focused specifically on the core value of a concise message and the power of visual storytelling to get a point across through narratives and visual storytelling. The small agency grew doing impactful work for major brands as well as large and small companies looking to clarify and simplify their message.

In 2013, Joe launched The BRIEF Lab (thebrieflab.com) after years dedicated to developing and delivering a unique curriculum on executive communication for the US Army Special Operations Command (Fort Bragg, North Carolina). The BRIEF Lab's mission is to teach not only military leaders but also professionals an elite standard of communication to improve operational efficiency and effectiveness.

Joe's first book, *BRIEF: Make a Bigger Impact By Saying Less* (Wiley, 2014), sets the standard for concise communication. His next book, *NOISE:*

*Living and Leading When Nobody Can Focus* (Wiley, 2019), addresses the devastating effects of information overload, digital devices, and nonstop distractions. His podcast, *Just Saying*, helps professionals become effective and efficient communicators in an age of information overload.

In 2022, Joe launched a new program called Quiet Works (www.quiet-works.com) to help professionals manage the noise in their lives by finding dedicated times and places for quiet. The first Quiet Workplace, an integrated, patented system to provide, promote, and protect quiet in the workplace, is now open in Southern Pines, North Carolina.

Before his entrepreneurial ventures, Joe served as senior vice president at Ketchum, a top-five marketing agency in Chicago, where he directed its corporate marketing practice and introduced new service models to enhance messaging and deepen relationships with market influencers.

Joe's clients include Microsoft, Mastercard, Grainger, Boeing, Harley-Davidson, Bank of America, JLL, and a variety of US military units and government organizations.

Joe received a BA in English literature from Loyola University Chicago, where he graduated with honors. He is fluent in Spanish and has broad international experience.

Joe and his wife, Julie, split their time between Southern Pines, North Carolina, and Chicago, Illinois. To learn more, please visit josephmccormack.com.

### About the Sheffield Company LLC

Founded in 2006, Sheffield is a privately held consulting and training organization that helps bring clarity to work. It was founded by Joe McCormack to help diverse organizations improve how they communicate and concentrate in a world filled with nonstop noise. The organization has two primary programs: The BRIEF Lab (www.thebrieflab.com) and the Quiet Workplace (www.thequietworkplace.com).

The following is an executive summary of the main courses and services Sheffield offers its corporate and government clients globally:

- **BRIEF 101:** the core methodology for clear and concise verbal communication.
- **BRIEF 102:** the core principles and practices for BRIEF writing skills.
- **BRIEF Meeting Facilitation:** the art and science of running meetings, online or in person.
- **BELT:** the BRIEF Experiential Learning Technique for developing exceptional instructors.
- **Quiet Works for Teams:** small cohorts create a culture of quiet in their organizations.
- **Quiet Works Off-sites:** semi-silent summits combine collaboration with time alone.
- **Quiet Works for Coaches:** a certification program for improving the coach–client relationship.
- **Quiet Works for [BRIEF] Teams:** small cohorts improve brevity with better preparation.

For more information, call 630-310-5190 or send an email directly to jmccormack@sheffieldcompany.com.